Perfect Marriage
Not a Mirage

A journey through ups and downs of marriage

Poonam A. Bamba

PUSTAK MAHAL®

Publishers
Pustak Mahal®
J-3/16, Daryaganj, New Delhi-110002
☎ 23276539, 23272783, 23272784 • *Fax:* 011-23260518
E-mail: info@pustakmahal.com • *Website:* www.pustakmahal.com

Sales Centre
- 10-B, Netaji Subhash Marg, Daryaganj, New Delhi-110002
  ☎ 23268292, 23268293, 23279900 • *Fax:* 011-23280567
  E-mail: rapidexdelhi@indiatimes.com
- Hind Pustak Bhawan
  6686, Khari Baoli, Delhi-110006, ☎23944314, 23911979

Branches
Bengaluru: ☎ 080 22234025 • *Telefax:* 080-22240209
E-mail: pustak@airtelmail.in • pustak@sancharnet.in
Mumbai: ☎ 022-22010941, 022-22053387
E-mail: rapidex@bom5.vsnl.net.in
Patna: ☎ 0612-3294193 • *Telefax:* 0612-2302719
E-mail: rapidexptn@rediffmail.com
Hyderabad: *Telefax:* 040-24737290
E-mail: pustakmahalhyd@yahoo.co.in

ISBN 978-81-223-1106-8

Edition: 2010

Printed at : Param Offsetters, Okhla, New Delhi-110020

This book is dedicated
to
the sacred relationship called 'marriage'

Let me not to the marriage of true minds
Admit impediments. Love is not love
Which alters when it alteration finds,
Or bonds with the remover to remove
O no, it is an ever-fixed mark
That looks on tempests and is never shaken;
It is the star to every wandering bark
Whose worth's unknown, although his height be taken.
Love's not Time's fool, though rosy lips and cheeks
Within his bending sickle's compass come;
Love alters not with his brief hours and weeks,
But bears it out, even to the edge of doom.
If this be error and upon me proved,
I never writ, nor no man ever loved.

William Shakespeare: Sonnets 116

CONTENTS

FROM THE HEART

Why am I writing this?

My tenure as an Additional District Judge, Matrimonial Court, brought me face to face with the reality of marital life. It was a God sent opportunity to observe the institution of marriage from such close quarters. I was interacting each day with human beings in different stages of misery, as they perceived themselves to be. I was experiencing trauma, without being a part of it. The number of divorce cases made me reflect deeply on why marriages fail.

Varied encounters, myriad of questions and dilemmas for which spouses looked up to me with great expectation and their search for a cicerone in me, made me work harder each day; it forced me analyse my own relationships – marital et al, every moment; what has made my own marriage work ? What is keeping it alive and interesting? Like a child I was hunting day and night for solutions to spouses' queries. Spouses' confidence in me added further to my burden. I was kind of swinging with the spouses; the emotional baggage unloaded by spouses, weighed me down on some occasions.

"He called me yesterday night; he begged of me to return to matrimonial home and promised that he would never raise his hand on me again. But I find it hard to believe him. What do you say? Do you think he deserves another chance? I will join him if you say" asked one wife. Such queries by the spouses left me speechless. I was humbled by the confidence reposed in me by such spouses. I would tell them that they have to weigh and decide for themselves; I can only present a complete picture before them and can guide them only to an extent. "Why am I telling that?" I would often ask myself immediately thereafter. "Decide" that is what they could not do; they were in quandary.

Confusion would be writ large on their faces; they wished to save their marriages but didn't know whether it was wise to give it another shot, after umpteenth attempts having already been made. I would feel like responding in the following manner as the cat did in "Alice in Wonderland".

"Would you tell me, please which way I ought to go from here?

'That depends a good deal on where you want to get to,' said the Cat.

'I don't much care where -,' said Alice.

'Then it doesn't matter which way you go,' said the Cat.

'- so long as I get somewhere,' Alice added as an explanation.

'Oh, you're sure to do that,' said the Cat, 'if you only walk long enough.'

Alice in Wonderland, Lewis Carroll.

The reasons for which spouses chose to split ranged from trivia to the unimaginable. Some situations were straight out of Hindi movies. Some were amusing and some appalling.

When I shared my experiences in the court with my colleagues and near and dear ones, their reactions revealed that they were as appalled or amused as I was. That is how I came to record in my diary, some of my encounters with husbands and wives of different hues and colors, which then took shape of this book "Perfect marriage - not a mirage".

My interaction with spouses revealed that it was really difficult to know the truth. I would often think, are both of them narrating their true experiences? Are they exaggerating? When I heard one spouse, I was completely convinced with his/ her story and could relate it to a real life experience. But when I spoke with the other spouse, his/ her side of the story also sounded quite real, which could also fit straight into any next door neighbour's story. Each would sound oppressed by the other. I would often be baffled, "who is the aggrieved spouse? With time, I came to realise that nobody is right or wrong. It's only a matter of perception. There is nothing "black" and "white". There is just a lot of grey. It is only a clash of two perceived realities — two views of the same situation. The husband will have his perception of the way things are between him and his wife, while she may have a completely different perception of the same.

Something which is seriously 'wrong' for one, may not be so for the other. Neither was dishonest. Both revealed their life story, as they perceived it. It was surprising to see, how the same incident was perceived so differently by two individuals. I really grew to understand that in life no one is wrong in one's own point of view.

There actually is no one reality. Every situation has so many aspects that one person's truth might be another's lie. Unless one has a vision that enables one to view the total reality, one is bound to be like the blind men who touched different parts of an elephant and called it a snake, tree-trunk or root, depending on which part of the elephant's body they touched. There is no absolute truth.

Nobody can understand the reality of a marriage except the husband and wife themselves. Even the couple doesn't understand the reality, because there is no one reality. Nothing can be totally wrong in this world. Even the stopped clock gives correct time twice a day.

I grew each day with unhappy spouses; my interaction with them helped me discover that satisfaction and happiness come from within. No one else can make us happy unless we want to be so. I also saw that money and matter did not guarantee marital bliss; both kinds of spouses, those who had all the riches of life and those who lacked material possessions, were unhappy. The rich suffered lack of warmth from their spouse. The poor felt that they could not bring up their children or survive only on love. Someone was aggrieved that the spouse was indifferent and did not take any responsibility. Another felt aggrieved as the spouse was too interfering. These experiences encouraged me to go beyond my (official) duty and delve deeper into each situation. I also started interacting with other people coming in my contact, to know how they felt about their marriage and divorce. I talked with people in different stages of marriage: from excitement-to- boredom-to divorce.

These encounters reaffirmed the fact that there is nothing like 'perfect match" or for that matter a perfect mother-in-law. As with any other relationship, marriage also calls for a lot of adjustment, a degree of compromise, and a lot of effort to turn it into a lasting partnership. The trouble starts with the search for the "perfect mate" and perfect "in-laws". I realised that to have a lasting relationship, one needs to respect not only one's spouse but also his/ her folks.

To build a pleasant relationship, a couple needs to give time to each other to adjust to the new company and to respect each other's way of life. Attempt to change the other is surely avoidable. It must not be forgotten for a moment that marriage is a union of two different personalities, who have chosen to spend rest of their lives together for their own reasons.

Many a conversation with divorced spouses revealed that the grass is not always greener on the other side. Therefore, a little patience and not rushing for divorce over minor maladjustments, thinking that one will be happy everafter, after the divorce might go a long way. Divorce is not a guarantee of perpetual bliss. Nobody is perfect, so one may as well look for the positive side of the person one is married to. Some of the stories in the book will reveal that the search for perfect love does not lead you anywhere. You may discover that the one you are now married to, (after divorce) has more imperfections than the one you left behind. So love the one you are with.

Divorce may be a way but not the only way.

I am not saying that divorce should not be considered, or that once married, you must stay in the marriage come what may. In some situations, divorce may be the only solution and sooner the better. It may be better to be separated than being in a "living hell" every day. There could be various reasons for separation, like drug abuse, alcoholism, constant torture: physical or mental, extra–marital affair etc. But there surely is a case for taking a closer look at your relationship before you snap ties. Weigh the positives and the negatives. If the positives exceed the negatives and some hope is left, one should not hesitate to give their marriage a chance. See a marriage counsellor. Repair work on marriage can only be done, while you are still married.

I came across such diverse reasons for divorce that I was convinced that there is no uniform code which can make a marriage work. There can be no 'perfect recipe' or "rule book" which can guide us to a successful marriage.

"The secret of happy marriage remains a secret."

— Henry Young Man.

But, we can surely learn something from the blunders committed by others. This book is an attempt to share my experiences with everyone so that some of us can avoid mistakes, which others made, without going through the mess others have gone through. This is an effort to share a thought that if you are heading for separation, take a closer look at what you are leaving. If there is even an iota of hope left, it might make sense to give your marriage a chance because separation, most of the times, proves disastrous for children.

It would give me an immense satisfaction if this work saves even a single relationship. I shall feel that somebody's trauma hasn't gone waste; its negative energy has been effectively directed towards positivity and has been instrumental in bringing about peace in someone else's life. A home saved would achieve a much larger purpose because harmony at home brings harmony in society, which in turn brings harmony in the nations; and harmony in the universe

"Perfect marriage : not a mirage" is a journey, from the "concept of marriage" to whether "perfect match – is a myth or reality" to "what ails marriage" and "how to save this relationship" and the "recent trends" seen in marriages in our country.

All the narrations in this book are real life stories, but names of the characters have been changed. Reading this book, I hope, will help you look at the institution of marriage with a different perspective and attitude. You may realise that perfection in a relationship can be attained with a little effort on both the sides.

***

1

THE BOND OF MARRIAGE

The Concept

"I have always considered marriage as the most interesting event of one's life, the foundation of happiness or misery."

— George Washington,
Letter to Burwell Bassett,
May 23,1785

Originally derived from French word "Mariage", the marriage or wedlock or the formal union of a man and a woman, by which they become man and wife, is the most revered as well as lamented upon institution in a society.

Marriage for some, is a spiritual bond; a union of two souls which is made in heaven but performed in the world. There are others, who believe that marriage is a customary arrangement for propagating one's lineage.

In India, marriage is sacred. It is not only a spiritual union of two individuals but also that of two families. The religious sanction to marriage, from as early as the time of Rig-Veda has heightened the character and importance of the institution of marriage.

In Hindu law, marriage is treated as a Samskāra or a sacrament. It is one of the important sacraments, enjoined by the Hindu religion for regeneration of men and obligatory in the case of every Hindu who does not desire to adopt the life of a Sanyāsi.

Of the eight forms of marriage recognised by the ancient Hindu Law, four were approved forms and four unapproved. Each form of marriage depicts a different stage of social progress. The Indian life presented almost every possible form of conjugal relation, from the grossest polyandry to the purest and the most rational form of monogamy as it exists today. Marriage in India is considered to be an amalgam of three important duties i.e. social, religious and spiritual. The significance attached to the institution of marriage even outside India can be guaged from the fact that in 1981, in view of the decline of the institution of marriage, couples in Baton Rouge, La., encouraged the Mayor, the Governor and the Bishop to proclaim "St. Valentine's Day" as "We believe in Marriage Day". The name of St. Valentine's Day designated to be celebrated each year on the second Sunday in February was then changed to "World Marriage Day"[1]. Given this context and background, the questions surrounding marriage today signify deep doubts about individual responsibilities.

Whether one should get married and get tied down or whether one should opt for the freedom of relationships without the bond of marriage, is a question often debated by the younger generation. This generation is weighing whether a lifetime commitment is too onerous and whether it is worth giving up one's freedom for. People debate whether the institution of marriage has lost its significance. Every now and then, a newspaper or a magazine publishes results of surveys about "marriage as an institution" to make a point that the younger generation does not attach as much importance to the institution of marriage, as it used to; and that "live-in" relationship is being preferred by the upwardly mobile younger generation.

If all this is true, then why do we still witness weddings at a scale more lavish than ever? What is it about wedding that makes people enact wild fantasies? As Bratten said, "Even though today's bride and groom are older and wiser, the hope and excitement about the wedding and getting married is still there. That means having a big, traditional wedding surrounded by family and friends, and saying time-honored vows; most often in a religious setting. There is still that feeling that a wedding is a major event in life that they are committing to one another for a lifetime."

Unique Preparations

There are "destination weddings" where couples say "I do" at exotic locales. Laxmi Mittal chose Versailles Palace as the venue for his daughter's wedding. People get married under the sea, on top of a bridge, in the sky and wherever else their imagination takes them: from the dunes of Rajasthan to the tea gardens of Darjeeling, from Himalayan Hill tops to private islands or the Virgin beaches of Goa.

Recently, a West Delhi based middle class father had put up a unique five feet high rotating 'jai mālā manch' (stage) where the bride and groom stood surrounded by the friends and relatives to garland each other. As the turntable rotated, all the guests got a clear view of the boy and girl. At the time of the jai mala, electric-blowers showered rose petals on the couple to simulate a "phool varshā" (rain of flowers); Jai-Jai Rām, Sitā Rām blared from the speakers, as the couple exchanged garlands. It was arranged to draw maximum advantage from the 'marriage made in heaven' view. That marriage was made to appear celestial. In his interview to a National Daily, the father shared with pride that he wanted to put up such a show at his daughter's wedding so that every guest would remember it for his/her entire life[2].

A Punjabi businessman from Sainik Farms sent 100 invitations worth Rs.1.5 lakh each. Following the IPL matches, a Marwari family from Baroda made a request to the organiser for the Washington Redskins to cheerlead their son's bārāt (wedding procession).

In Sydney, Australia, a British couple had a "wedding with a view", when they had their marriage ceremony on the top of Sydney Harbour Bridge. They braved the cold wind and damp to climb some 440 ft. above the harbour, to be the first to get married on the famous icon with a spectacular view. The bride's wedding ring was also attached to a safety rope, just in case something went wrong[3].

Very recently, a New York City couple touched yet another height. They floated into matrimony thousands of feet above Gulf of Mexico, to be the world's first couple to have weightless wedding held in zero gravity conditions aboard specially modified Boeing 727-200 aircraft, G-Force one; it was operated by the Zero Gravity Corp or Zero-G, a company offering weightless flight experiences. The bridegroom, who wanted to do something different, had organized the feat. He shared with press that his tuxedo tails were specially stiffened, so that they do not float out of control. He admitted that he had trouble lining up his lips for the all-important wedding kiss. He said "Noah knocked into my nose and I thought it would bleed." We have now spawned wedding coordinators and wedding consultants to put up marital extravaganzas.

Significance Attached to Marriage Ceremonies

According to industry estimates, every year close to 600 exotic weddings take place in India at palatial mansions and other exclusive locales. We see films from HAHK to KHNH showing big marriage sequences; there are umpteen number of tele serials such as "Dulhan", "Sapnā Babul Kā', 'Bidāi" etc. depicting significance of marriage. If media and our films depict even an iota of what touches the emotions of general public, it reflects, that "wedding" is still considered to be a major life event and that couples are making life time commitments with a great deal of fanfare.

So much of significance being attached to marriage reiterates its social relevance. The need to belong to a given social structure which binds not only the couple but also gives name and standing to many other relationships attained through this association, confers on marriage its distinct flavour and sanctity.

Promises by Var and Vadhu during Marriage

In India as a part of marriage rituals each Var (Groom) and Vadhu (Bride) take some vows.

Var-Pratigyā: O my rightfully wed wife! From now on we have become one as you have been declared my better half. I accept you in the most important role of grihalakshmi (the goddess of wealth of the household; the mistress of the house) and declare that I will do everything with your consent. Before the Fire God and all the persons present here, I resolve that I will always remain soft, flexible, delicate and tolerant. Even when you would be weak or distracted from duties, you would get my faith and cooperation. You will always get my loving words; true behaviour and penance-like sincerity of one devoted to a single wife. I will run the household on righteous path on your advice and with your consent. Even when there is some difference of opinion or something wrong with the deeds, I would peacefully follow the righteous path.

Vadhu Pratigyā:

"O my god! I have had the good fortune of acquiring you with the merits that I accumulated by various deeds in different births.

"I'll look after your entire family from children to the aged and will be happy with whatever is available as sustenance.

"I'll timely prepare delicious food and follow your orders and directives.

"I'll embellish myself with clean clothes and jewellery and indulge with you in physical pleasure with body, mind and spirit.

"I'll face sorrow bravely and bloom during happy days. I'll share pleasure and pain with you and never indulge in adultery.

"I'll perform all your household chores with pleasure. I'll serve the father-in-law, and all other relatives. I'll be with you wherever you are. I'll never deceive you.

"I'll assist you in all religious rites and rituals, and homa, obey you in righteous deeds, accumulation of wealth and fulfillment of desire. Here in the presence of Agnideva, Brāhmins and relatives, you have become my husband, and I offer my body to you."

Marriage would be bliss if these wedding promises are followed in letter and spirit.

Love marriage Vs Arranged marriage / My choice : Their choice

The debate continues over love marriage versus arranged marriage. Is it better to marry a person selected by one's parents? Or would it be better to get to know somebody before getting into a long term alliance? Or should one go in for "a love cum arranged marriage".

There appears to be no single success formula. I have seen even those marriages fail, which were arranged after perfectly matching the horoscopes and after making every possible enquiry about the boy, the girl and their respective families. I have also seen the collapse of marriages contracted after courtship of a decade or more.

"Happiness in marriage is entirely a matter of chance. If the dispositions of the parties are ever so well known to each other or ever so similar beforehand, it does not advance their felicity in the least. They always

continue to grow sufficiently unlike afterwards to have their share of vexation; and it is better to know as little as possible of the defects of the person with whom you are to pass your life."

Jane Austen, Pride and Prejudice

Long courtship - no guarantee

There was a couple, which got married after friendship of about ten years. Cracks in their relationship set in within one year of marriage. The wife shared "being good friends for such a long time, the decision to part ways was not easy; but it was a choice they had to make, as there was no point in clinging on to the relationship which simply was not working."

Everyone has his/her own concept of marriage. Each relationship is unique and so are its reasons for working or not working. In yet another case of a socialite, who divorced her husband after 12 years of love marriage shared, "I was married at 18 and divorced at 35. I practically grew up with Gautam, but somewhere we fell out of love.... we simply started having too many issues which didn't seem to get solved even after a considerable period of time. I discussed the issues with Gautam and we came to a mutual agreement that we would give our marriage our best for a year. And if our equation remained the same even then, we would part ways and remain friends. We stuck to our agreement. After all, think about it: how much time do you truly spend with your husband? In a day, two or three hours maximum! You spend more time at your work place, with kids, with friends, commuting, et al. Yet this relationship means the most. So, if you're putting in that kind of effort, why invest in a wrong relationship?"

Marriage has been known to be a gamble. No one knows whether a beautiful bride from a well known family, would make a dutiful and understanding wife or a loving and caring mother; whether the wonderful son of your long time friend would make a good husband for your daughter. Because, as soon as the knot is tied, the equation changes. Romance is replaced by understanding and companionship or by bickering and bitterness. Life comes down from the highs of romance to a more ordinary and humdrum existence which may become difficult to come to terms with.

Impulsive love marriage meets the same fate

An impulsive "love marriage" of Sumangla, a young girl fell apart soon after the romantic high wore off.

18 years old Sumangla belonged to a refined Bengali family. Sumangla became close to a college mate's brother Sumit Grover. Sumit aged about 29 years, belonged to a very well to do Punjabi business family. When Sumangla was in the final year of her BA, her father got transferred to Delhi. She stayed back at Kolkata to complete her graduation. Sumangla and Sumit came closer around this time. Sumangla found a fun loving companion in Sumit, who also happened to be a handsome man. She was so enamoured by his good looks and trendy bike that she decided to marry him, while she was yet to complete her graduation. They dated for about two years. After her final examinations got over, Sumangla called up her mother and told her that she had decided to marry a 'Punjabi' boy. Sumangla's father reacted predictably. "Come back home. We will find you much better boys". This reaction made Sumangla panic. She thought that she would not be allowed to meet Sumit again, if she returned to her parents. So, Sumangla, at the age of 18½ years, got married without her parents' blessings to Sumit, who was more than 10 years older to her. Reluctantly, with the passage of time, Sumangala's parents accepted the marriage.

Marriage brought Sumangla face to face with life. Initially, she found it to be good fun. But, steadily she found that her fun loving husband had a loud way of talking, typical Punjabi mannerism and no interest in fine arts or culture or any other thing except food. Sumangla realised that they were poles apart, temperamentally.

Sumangla confided, "I did not like his ways. Naively, I thought I will teach him some social graces, which I felt he lacked. He pretended willingness to give it a shot. But that was only superficial. We started drifting apart....I started avoiding inviting my friends in his presence..... Neither would he like my going out too much, though finances were never a problem. He would always provide me with funds.... but somewhere I was feeling annihilated. I was restless and wanted to be freed. I could not speak to my parents for the fear of their backlash: "We told you so". It was my decision so I had to live with it.

I conceived my son after about three years of marriage. Things started looking up again. I came to my parents' house at Delhi for delivery. During that period, I got to hear that in my absence Sumit was seeing other woman and spending a lot of money on gambling. On my return, a facade was put up. Things were made to look normal. But, he continued seeing some other woman. That was the turning point, when I decided to quit. But I was not confident, whether I would be able to handle life on my own. I was a simple graduate. Having made up my mind, I picked up a job as an office assistant. Sumit thought, it was a fad and I would get over that. I gained confidence. Then all my efforts were directed towards creating my own niche. With the help of my friends at Delhi, a job and a house was arranged at Delhi. Then I took my parents into confidence. I casually went for a holiday to Delhi along with my son and the servant in the usual course. I got my son admitted in a school at Delhi before returning to Kolkata. I told Sumit that I had decided to snap the relationship. He resisted a little, but could not really stop me. I left my matrimonial home with just one small suitcase. I did not demand any financial support from him.

I filed a divorce case after about three years of our separation. Divorce was granted ex-parte, as Sumit did not join the proceedings....."

When I asked her, whether she regretted, having not listened to her parents? She said ".... I did regret... but I think, had my parents not said 'no' so strictly and had they explained to me and handled me little more tactfully, I would not have rebelled and gone ahead to marry Sumit, at the age of 18 ½ years..."

Sumangla's panic reaction may also find explanation in human physiology. Anthropologist Helen Fisher in her book "Anatomy of Love" claims that this urgency to unite is wired into our brain chemistry. Fisher writes, "This violent emotional disturbance that we call infatuation (or attraction) may begin with a small molecule called phenylethylamine, or PEA. Known as the excitant amine, PEA is a substance in the brain that causes feelings of elation, exhilaration, and euphoria.

Whether infatuation is induced by chemicals or mystically inspired, once bitten and smitten, we are aflame. The fury of love springs from the soul, and therefore, cannot be doused by free will or rationale.

... it is not a high that is biologically sustainable, as other chemicals kick in and lust turns into attachment..."

Fisher puts the normal duration of infatuation stage as two or three years and the peak time for a couple to divorce tends to be in the fourth year of the relationship.

Iris Krasnow in "Surrendering to Marriage" warns, "Because we are designed to fall in love but not stay that way, we must resist our natural, animal restlessness with the sheer force of our human will power.

... We'll be flooded with new brain chemicals that could turn Mr. Dream Machine into a boring schmuck. We need to keep remembering that nothing real can ever throb like the psychedelic dance in our imaginations, that fantasy is fantasy, and reality is what's really going on."

But Sumangla found out the hard way that it does not make sense to plunge into marriage, just to prove your point, or out of panic that others might prevent you from going ahead. Before tying the knot, it might be wise to ask oneself - Is this just an infatuation? Is there something other than the real person which has attracted you? The family can help and provide you the space and time to decide whether you are making the right choice. As Sumangla said with hindsight that had her parents not objected so strongly, she may not have made the mistake of a hasty marriage. Parents also need to separate their own sense of shock and disapproval from the choice made by their children and need to give them time and space to arrive at their own decisions.

Kiran on similar path despite long courtship

There are cases in stark contrast to that of Sumangla, where a couple going steady for as long as a decade still ended up in a failed marriage. Kiran and Amit were going steady since 12th standard. Their courtship continued for about 8 years. Kiran completed her post graduation. Amit struggled to get a job. They tied the knot after Amit got a job. Within 2-3 months of their marriage, trouble started brewing. There would be bickering on every small thing. Amit, when asked during counseling, the reason of so much bickering said, "I don't know? She picks up a fight on anything and everything. She is not ready to take up any responsibility. If I tell her to make even a cup of tea, she retorts with "earlier you would run and prepare tea, whenever I visited. Can't you do that now? ..... She wants to go out for a movie.... to eat outside every weekend. It doesn't work that way when you are living in a joint family. But she is not ready to understand. She thinks we are still (the) love birds and can fly whenever and wherever we want."

When Kiran was asked, as to what went so wrong that their courtship of eight years had come crashing down in two months of marriage, her response was, "No romance is left in our relationship, he just pushes me away, even if I put my arm around his neck. Earlier he would not lose a single opportunity to kiss and hug me. Every weekend and holiday, he would pester me for going out for a movie, visiting new restaurants. He literally worshipped me, never criticised me and was ready to do anything and everything for me. But now, if I ask him for going out, he gets irritated..... He keeps preaching about my responsibilities. ....we are like snarling animals in a cage ready to tear each other apart...... I think love has simply vanished from our relationship..... God knows what went so terribly wrong after we got married. I can't believe myself that I loved "this" person for 8 long years. I always thought, I knew Amit very well. But now I find him a total 'stranger'. I can't stand the sight of this stranger, any more."

Counselling sessions also could not help resolve their differences.

When you are dating, you have no agenda other than to make each other happy. In marriage, there are many other issues to be addressed all the time; *keeping each other happy is not the top or the only priority.*

Kiran, I think measured her "love and romance" by the number of outings and the quantum of pampering by Amit. She probably did not see the point that with this relationship called "marriage", come certain responsibilities. You can't behave like love birds all the time. Amit perhaps could not maintain the fine balance; he brought Kiran to earth straight from heaven. He started preaching only about her responsibilities, and dropped all the romance.

Romance and responsibilities can very well go hand-in-hand.

Kiran's dreams and fantasies came crashing. She could not understand and accept the transformed personality of Amit and felt shortchanged. She developed self doubts and often asked herself –'Did she really love this person? Did she ever actually know this person?'

Marriage does change the equation between couples. One needs to be prepared for this change and to accept that certain parts of the relationship will change. But it is still possible to remain friends after marriage. You may have to put in some effort to keep the friendship alive, give adequate space to your partner to be himself/herself and not fall into pre-conditioned roles. Shabana Azmi recently shared - "we are the best of friends; even marriage failed to ruin our friendship! We share the same world, and yet give each other enough space. I rely very heavily on Javed for his intellectual inputs." Javed Akhtar added, "We have sobering effect on each other. For example, if I am thinking too passionately or reacting rather too emotionally, she will be there to sober me down and quite often, the roles are reversed. So we are sitting on a seesaw!"

Marriage is a delicate balancing of needs and choices of both the spouses. It is not a contest of who is going to win the round. The peculiarities of the spouse, which become more pronounced as one ages, have to be respected even though you may not like them.

The key to a successful relationship lies more in the value one gives to one's relationship, be it with a spouse or a partner ; it is important to invest in that togetherness. The greatest threat to the partnership is the demand of individual space that partners make of each other. The moment this demand overtakes, it is the testing times for the relationship.

Our Pledge

We pledge to each other to be loving friends and partners in marriage;

To talk and to listen, to trust and appreciate one another;

To respect and cherish each other's uniqueness;

To support, give comfort and strengthen each other through life's joys and sorrows.

We promise to share hopes, thoughts and dreams as we build our lives together.

May our lives be ever intertwined, our love keeping us together!

We will build a home that is compassionate to all.

We will show respect and honor to others and each other.

May our home be forever filled with peace, happiness and love!

Sometimes marriage fails, even after a long courtship and there are no answers to what went wrong. Courtship does help to know the other person, at least enough to avoid nasty surprises after marriage. But sometimes people maintain illusions about each other even during long courtships and one may not get to know the real person. Pre-marital courtship and a long affair, therefore, is no guarantee to a happy and lasting marriage.

You marry a lover and watch him change into a stark stranger; and someone marries a stranger and grows to love him/her over years. You never know what is in store.

Why marriages still break, though contracted after long association and courtship, has found a scientific explanation.

Chemistry of the bond

Michael Gurian in his article titled "The Science of Happy Marriage"[4] beautifully discussed chemistry behind falling in love and falling apart after marriage. He has explained that when two lovers come together their brains begin to "fall in love". The couple's pheromones – chemical signals that work throughout senses – are very high. So, when they smell each other or look into each other's eyes, their separate male and female minds become like one. High levels of oxytocin, a bonding hormone, may hide irritating behaviours from each other. That is "Romance." But lovers' bliss ultimately ends, and a new biological stage of the relationship begins after marriage.

Then "disillusionment" begins. After a few months or even an year, hormones and brain chemistry begins to change, and the "thinking brain" – the cerebral cortex may notice that the partner is flawed. The couple then feels anger towards each other, along with irritation, even fear at times. If we married our partner during the "Romance" stage, we might, in Stage 2, begin to have second thoughts.

But this confusing phase is a normal stage, a chemical let down in both their brains. It's also a necessary step in helping two very different brain systems come together for life.

Then the "Power Struggle" begins. Two people who experience "disillusionment" will usually initiate "Power Struggle". They will counter the invisible chemical let down by trying to change each other back to: who they were, or thought they were-in the "Romance" stage.

Next stage is "Awakening." Before drifting apart, there comes a stage which goes unnoticed. After "Romance", "Disillusionment" and "Power Struggle", the man and woman become too close, erasing one another's individuality. A man might see his wife's emotionality, need to communicate, desire for sensual romance and even attitude towards house work as a waste of time. She might see her husband's habits, hobbies, pre-occupation with work and need for independence as dangerous and selfish. In this 4th state, the couple awakens to the realisation that they have been too close to each other's unhealthy ways and must now psychologically separate. The separation does not mean divorce. It means understanding. In this new state, the thinking brain overrides emotional responses that could cause conflict and a feeling of grief over their lost romance. A man might step back and say nothing when he sees his wife doing something that irritates – he just mentally steps around it. A woman might supportively say, "I get what that's about now," when he does something equally irritating to her.

Ultimately men realise that women are right. A relationship is most likely to be doomed if there isn't enough togetherness. But men are right, too. It is most likely to be in a serious trouble, if there is not enough independence.

When we are too far away from each other, that amazing love we knew at the beginning will die. Yet, when we are so close that one person will not allow the other to be him or herself, the marriage can't survive. Understanding the strengths of male and female chemistry is the key to success.

The chemistry of bonding and un-bonding gives a deep insight into the process of love fructifying into marriage and staying on course. In a 'Long-Term Marriage' couples live together, raise children, love and are loved, not because they've become the same as each other, but because they've learned to be happily different.

The Prophet

Love one another, but make not a bond of love:
Let it rather be a moving sea between the shores of your souls.
Fill each other's cup but drink not from one cup.
Give one another of your bread but eat not from the same loaf.
Sing and dance together and be joyous,
But let each one of you be alone:
Even as the strings of a lute are alone
Though they quiver with the same music.
Give your hearts, but not into each other's keeping;
For only the hand of life can contain your hearts.
And stand together yet not too near together:
For the pillars of the temple stand apart,
And the oak tree and the cypress grow not in each other's shadow.

—Khalil Gibran

There are as many successful "love" marriages as those, which fail. So is true of "arranged" marriages.

Sunny side of arranged marriage

An arranged marriage might have an edge over love marriage, in case serious differences arise between the husband and wife. In that situation, families step in to resolve the issue, which may not be the case in love marriage. Love marriages in our country, generally take place without the parents' consent and the couples in difficult situations are less likely to seek help of their respective families.

'Arranged marriage' has yet another sunny side. You learn new things about your partner everyday and this keeps the novelty of the relationship alive for long. A love marriage may not have much room for surprises. But arranged marriage also has its own negatives. It requires plenty of adjustments and compromises. The burden of adjusting with the husband's family in our social milieu is primarily that of the bride.

The younger generation in India is now insisting that they must know the person before they get married. It is amusing to note that in contrast, Britons are getting lessons in how the principles of arranged marriage could help strengthen their increasingly complicated relationships through a new television programme, "Arrange me a Marriage" on National Terrestrial BBC-2. Aneela Rehman, the anchor of the show, gives tips on how to find a long-term partner. Many of the persons who featured on the programme had pursued relationship with incompatible partners whose family backgrounds and aspirations did not match with their own.[5] People abroad still carry some confusion about the difference between arranged marriage and forced marriage. They find it hard to understand how young-persons can willingly agree to marry total strangers.

When crossing across becomes your cross

Priyanka Todi, a Hindu girl belonging to a rich business family and Rizwanur, a Muslim who had struggled from the slums of Tiljala to become a graphic designer and teacher, captured the nation's attention for weeks together. The couple was trapped between their desire to be married, the rights guaranteed by the law and their socio cultural reality. Priyanka was restored to her Hindu family, after Rizwanur was found dead on train tracks in Kolkata. It took death to draw them apart. Could Rizwanur after coming this far ever have predicted that his pure/ innocent love would have cost him his life?

In feudal literature romantic love was essentially anti social and adulterous. But I used to carry the impression that our society, particularly the educated urbanised section of society, has become more liberal and has come to accept inter-caste and inter-religious marriages; that it was now common for people to cross these traditional barriers and come together in marriage, and the older generation eventually relented and accepted cross-cultural marriages. I happily lived with this impression till I encountered poignant stories to the contrary.

Assertion of their choice by a couple belonging to different religions is seen as a direct attack on parental authority, community, social norms and religious beliefs. Why are we so fixed in our thinking? Why in our quest to preserve the so called "honour", we resort to the most dishonourable deeds.

"Honour killings" are a particularly gruesome aspect of the assertion of parental and community authority. The perceived slur which falls on the "honour" of the family or community when couples marry or create a relationship against the wishes of the family, is often avenged by cold blooded murder. The fact that perfectly sane, normal and educated people can also indulge in this crime has been a matter of growing concern for the last few years. In yet another case, Bharti Yadav's relationship with Nitish Katara was seen as a 'shame' on her "family honor". Nitish Katara was brutally murdered.

Those who breached the social norms faced disapproval, resistance, violence and at times death. Tremendous courage and determination is required to sail through an inter-caste and inter-religious love affair, to get married and then for the couple to survive because, the family of the girl often makes every effort to frame the boy alleging kidnapping, abduction and rape. The girl is coaxed, coerced and emotionally blackmailed to do her parents' bidding.

Away from the sensationalism of murders and killings, when normal people muster the courage to brave the community and family disapproval, and settle down into marriage, the marriage can yet be derailed by their family, as happened in the case of Ranjeet and Humera.

Humera succumbed to parents' pressure

Both Ranjeet and Humera were doing MBBS internship at a Govt. Hospital in Delhi. Ranjeet belonged to a Punjabi family based at Delhi. Humera was a Muslim girl, from Aligarh. Humera's father was also a doctor practising in Aligarh. Work brought Ranjeet and Humera together. They decided to get married after their short courtship during internship. All friends and colleagues advised Humera to carefully consider everything before going ahead with marriage. All through, Humera was firm that she was an educated adult and found no problem in getting married to a Hindu; If need be, she could withstand her parents' pressure against the alliance. Humera changed her religion and got married to Ranjeet at a simple ceremony in a temple at Delhi. They got their marriage registered with the help of their friends. They went for their honeymoon to Shimla. Humera broke the news of her marriage to her parents through a letter. As expected, her parents were shocked and refused to accept the marriage. When intimidation did not work, they began persuading her to come home to take their blessings.

After a month or so came Eid. Humera's brother called up Ranjeet and told him that all of them were missing her very much. He requested Ranjeet to let Humera visit them on the pious occasion of Eid. Ranjeet and Humera were emotionally moved. On the eve of Eid, Ranjeet let Humera accompany her brother for visiting her parents at Aligarh. That was the last time Ranjeet saw Humera.

Humera was not allowed to make phone calls or move out of the house. She was locked inside her room by her parents. Humera's parents arranged Humera's marriage with a Muslim boy. Humera's father threatened to commit suicide, if she did not agree to the marriage. Humera was married off to a Muslim boy of her parents' choice.

Ranjeet filed a writ of habeas corpus in Delhi High Court and thereafter, a petition for restitution of conjugal rights. During the proceedings, Humera denied her marriage with Ranjeet. She deposed before the court that marriage photographs produced by Ranjeet were that of a drama enacted by them in a college function. Ranjeet was shattered.

It is tragic that even today, in our country, the family does not accept a young adult's right to make decisions about his or her life, particularly in the case of girls. Despite all the education and modern outlook, when it comes to the marriage decision, the family may turn surprisingly regressive in outlook. Even today, inter-religious marriages are not easily accepted by parents, specially the girl's parents. There still exists an exaggerated and misplaced sense of honour in the Indian society. Women are still considered the repositories and vehicles of men's honour. Women must therefore, be regulated and disciplined so that men can strut their honour. By marrying without her parents' consent and that too a Hindu, Humera slighted her family's honour. Could Humera have thought that she would be made a hostage by her own parents for their honour and would be married off forcefully, ignoring her marital status?

The families, in such cases, cruelly ignore the emotional trauma they put the girl through, by pulling her out of one relationship and forcing her into another one. Ironically, the family honour is unaffected by the fact that the girl's own sense of honour and self-esteem may be torn to shreds.

Love marriage is not for weak hearts

Love marriages generally being against parents' wishes, call for immense endurance.

Do you wish to follow your heart? If you must, then do it with the inner strength of your mind. Be prepared to withstand parental pressure and emotional blackmail. A midway switchover can be a traumatic burden that you may carry for the rest of your life.

Of course, the stories are not always grim. Some sweethearts with firm heads do have their way. Mehrunissa was working as a computer engineer in a multinational company. She found a great companion in Rajan, a Tamil Brahmin. The camaraderie between them blossomed into a fragrant relationship. Both ultimately decided to tie the knot. Mehrunissa knew that her parents would never consent to her marriage with a Hindu. Both went ahead and got married at a simple ceremony in a temple with the help and support of a few trusted friends.

Quite expectedly, Mehrunissa's parents were shell shocked to learn about her marriage. The saving grace was that Mehrunissa's parents did not haunt her. They disowned her and did not try to find out her whereabouts. Her brother did get in touch with her over phone. When his trump card that their father had suffered a heart attack did not work, he extended subtle threats. But when Mehrunissa made it clear that she was serious about her relationship, her brother hung up and never called again.

Though Rajan's parents were also not at ease with this alliance initially, but they came to accept Rajan's decision reluctantly. They let Mehrunissa and Rajan stay in their flat despite their worst apprehensions about retaliation by Mehrunissa's parents.

Mehrunissa won Rajan's parents' hearts with her congenial disposition. Mehrunissa informed her mother about her conception, after about six months of her marriage. Mehrunissa's mother desired to meet her but not at her in-laws house. Mehrunissa after taking her parents-in-law into confidence went to meet her mother at a restaurant.

Mehrunissa was blessed with a baby boy. Her brother visited them on this occasion. Her parents however, did not visit her but congratulated her, her in-laws and Rajan over phone.

It had been three years since Mehrunissa married Rajan. Her relationship with her parents was almost back to normal but for the fact that they didn't visit her ever at her in-laws house. She was fine with that.

Having made up her mind, Mehrunissa pulled through the trauma of break-up with her parents.

Once the decision is taken, trust your instincts and follow your heart and soul with the strength at your command. Such alliances are not meant for weak hearts and minds. For those who cannot stay firm in their decisions, it is better to control their desire rather than subjecting themselves, their companions and parents to embarrassment, ridicule, and heartbreak which may end in serious consequences.

Caste: a shadow

Young couples, when headlong in love, do not find the caste and religion of one's partner worth considering. Sometimes, they are rudely shocked by society's attitude, and at other times, their own attitudes come in the way. Many people are fortunate enough to sail through parental and community opposition and settle down into married life. But then, their own cultural difference may come in the way and lead to problems.

Be it style of dressing, eating habits, rituals, festivals, language or mindset, you can take on the family only when you are yourself convinced that your spouse has the freedom to practice his or her own way of life. Inability to understand this was the reason Laxmi landed in the family court.

Laxmi was a high caste Kannadiga Brahmin and Nandu, a low caste Hindu from Patna. Both were lawyers by profession. They fell in love while working with a senior advocate at Supreme Court, and decided to get married. Laxmi wanted some time to convince her parents but Nandu was impatient. Ultimately, he persuaded Laxmi to get married at an Ārya Samāj Mandir and to register their marriage. Laxmi gave in and agreed for the marriage subject to the condition that they would keep it a secret till she convinced her parents. After their marriage, both continued with their normal life. Laxmi continued to stay with her parents, Nandu at his rented accommodation. Nandu restrained himself for sometime, but then started pressurising Laxmi to join him. Laxmi wanted some more time. Laxmi then disclosed her marriage to her sister and was waiting for an opportune time to break this news to her parents. Laxmi was however, put off by Nandu's constant nagging to join him at the earliest. Steadily, Laxmi also discovered that Nandu had many responsibilities including financial ones, towards his family settled in Patna. Nandu's father had retired and his five sisters were yet to be married. Nandu was the sole earner. Laxmi felt cheated that it was never revealed by Nandu earlier. Nandu's point was, "what has my family constitution to do with our affair and marriage. I never cheated on Laxmi; there was never an occasion to discuss all these things. I did not know, she was so money minded."

Laxmi's parents were not open to her marrying a low caste Hindu. Laxmi was also irritated by Nandu's insistence to join him soon. Moreover, after coming to know about Nandu's endless responsibilities, she lost the will and energy to fight her parents. Her mind was clouded by self doubt, whether she would be able to adjust to the ways of life of a 'low caste Hindu'? Would she be able to face her orthodox relatives? Laxmi then took a "reasoned" decision that the "fight" with her parents was not worth it.

But having married Nandu, she had to apply for divorce. Nandu was devastated. Laxmi also had to undergo a legal rigmarole. Laxmi wished that she had taken a "reasoned" decision instead of plunging into this alliance at her heart's dictates.

Where youngsters lack clarity and wisdom, parents can often help and guide them in the decision making. But parents have their own issues, their own fears and conditioning about sense of honour, sense of right and wrong, sense of what should be allowed and disallowed. A clear idea, as to what one is looking for in "marriage" might go a long way. Trouble can surely be avoided, if the priorities and choices are clear in the beginning itself.

Case after case revealed that the impulsive, spur of the moment decisions led to much grief. Marriage is too huge a commitment to be decided on whims.

Marriage, whether arranged or otherwise, can be a beautiful companionship, with a little adjustment on both the sides. It calls for an equitable give and take. It's a harmonious balance of complementary forces. A small commitment goes a long way.

I Love You

I love you
You are my best friend
Today, I give myself to you in marriage.
I promise to encourage and inspire you
To laugh with you, and to comfort you
In times of sorrow and struggle
I promise to love you in good times and in bad
When life seems easy and when it seems hard
When our love is simple, and when it is an effort

I promise to cherish you
And to always hold you in the highest regard
These things I give to you now;
And, promise to give all the days of our life.

—Unknown Poet

***

♥ Marriage is a beautiful relationship, where two individuals come together to form a union, becoming an inseparable part of each others' lives. The partners take care of each others' needs for the rest of their lives with mutual devotion, dignity and respect.

♥ True love can never hold you back it rather sets you free. You are happy in the happiness of the person you love unconditionally.

♥ There is no single formula for success of marriage ; arranged marriages can work great ; and love marriages can fail. Reverse is equally true.

♥ Impulsive plunge in love alliance to prove a point is surely avoidable. Marriage is too huge a commitment to be entered into, on a whim.

♥ Once you follow your heart, do it with the strength of your soul; such alliances are not for weak hearts.

♥ A little effort on both sides goes a long way.

2

PERFECT MARRIAGE: NOT A MIRAGE

Expectations give way to disillusionment. It is what leads to anguish, disappointment and grief. In the kaleidoscope of colours, so much was meant to be seen, to search and achieve... yet when one reached the desired destination it was just a colour combination which had a rainbow effect. A distant view of marriage also portrays only the shades of romance, variety and eternal spring of joy and happiness. When these shades merge to reflect the marital obligations, which call for constant efforts to measure up to the expectations of one and all in the marital home, one is jolted out of one's dream of eternal bliss.

Then, the inevitable question comes: Oh! Is the fountain spring the same which I thought would be the incessant source of eternal fulfillment and freedom of soul?

In any other relationship, we take our own time to decide the extent of involvement we should have; we may just decide to gradually move on if things are not to our liking, slowly sidestepping. Whereas, in marriage, whether "arranged" or "short term alliance fructifying into marriage", there is hardly any time to know the person. One has to accept the partner, as found. Marriage, in a way begins with acceptance of the bond, without an "exit" option. In this situation, when one enters matrimony, as if one is entering a fantasy land, one is certainly in for a shock on any unpleasant happening or on revelation of any unpleasant characteristic of the spouse. It then immediately comes to mind – "Is it worth continuing? Understanding that the marriage is a relationship, which has to be cultivated and nurtured after the nuptial bond, makes this bond beautiful.

Preamble: The marriage must work

I take you as my partner
I take you as my partner, my friend and my love
My hopes and dreams will now be intermingled with yours
I will seek to balance my needs with
Those of our community and family
I will openly draw from our combined experience
And feelings in our search for truth and meaning
I will strive for harmony through
Compromise and understanding.

—Unknown Poet

The earlier generations hardly had any time and luxury to dwell on their relationship too much. They stayed married because they were supposed to. That mindset made adjustment easier. They entered matrimony with a thought of permanence and stability. Quitting was not an option, usually. To provide a stable home for children was more important than the quality of their relationship. Wives were happy, enjoying motherhood and tending to family; husbands remained busy in their domain of bread-earner; they hardly spent time on measuring each others' imperfections. The woman had her own domain, and did not feel the need to share much with the man. The concept of feminism was not too familiar.

"By the end of the Sixteenth Century, love and marriage was already established as an important theme in literature.... marriage was tolerance and mutual survival in a couple of rooms, where winter was longer than summer and dearth more likely than plenty. The disastrous step to marriage as the end of the story, and the assumption of 'living happily ever after' had not yet been taken...."

Germaine Greer in "The Female Eunuch"

New frontiers

In last more than two decades, the woman has come to identify her rights and has started expressing her expectations. Fulfillment as a couple has become more pronounced. No doubt, this is an improvement over one's self-contentedness around oneself but paradoxically each feels entitled to life of "have it all" and to hold each other totally responsible for fulfilment or non-fulfilment in marriage. Spouses now believe that they can have tremendous excitement all through their life, which is a difficult state to attain. Non-fulfilment of unattainable leads to frustration and heart break.

Blurring boundaries in role models and at the same time, the continuance of conservativeness and attachment of the same importance to the traditional values has not only caused confusion but has also brought turmoil to the fragile beginnings of marital relationship. A man today basks in the glory of his wife's professional success but at the same time he wants her not only to play the house-maker but also to excel at it. You can't have it all! Not that the wife must embrace the strait jacket of a domestic role and subservience to the husband. But, the clear boundaries of each others' domains earlier made roles easier to adopt.

It is also not uncommon today to hear a spouse seeking his/ her space. Spouses now want value for their money. Both, men and women, look for a partner, which fits into their "model "and meet the "minimum specifications". Earlier, once the family of the boy/ girl was found to be decent and girl/ boy roughly matched the educational and professional status of the spouse, other features were not given much importance. Even after marriage not much attention was paid to other aspects. Now after marriage, each partner starts measuring the other at his/ her own scale of minimum.

The poet Dylan said, "People fall in love with a person's body.... with the way they dress, with their scorecards. With everything but their real selves, that is what you need to love if you wish to be happy together."

Marriage is a tough life Situation.

The institution of marriage needs to be worked on. Couples these days no longer want to work on their marriage and head for divorce at the drop of the hat. Iris has beautifully put it -

> "Marriage means tortuous work and a predictable routine; that's what you should expect. Indeed, a successful marriage has little to do with sustained bliss and everything to do with

> surrendering to the grind. When you ask yourself "is this all there is?" about the spouse you've been sharing a bathroom with for ten or thirty or fifty years, there's a good chance the answer is yes, this is it – jackhammer snoring, a man who watches too much sports, a husband who will never change. But if you look hard at what you also have – great kids, a loyal partner, a family unit as an anchor – usually you will discover that all that is yours, however imperfect, is more than enough....
>
> ... We still get in bad tiffs, but over time we have learned not to run from each other, we stay in the cage ; we are a family, we have to where would we go?
>
> Iris Krasnow in "Surrendering to Marriage"

Globalisation, the economic independence of women and the general shift towards individualism and materialism has made everyone more demanding. Consumerism as a philosophy reinforces the idea of "individual choice". It provides legitimacy to fulfilling the same and keeping "individual choice" above the "common choice". Spouses today are very demanding of their partners. If the relationship does not work, people do not take much time to make exit.

Personal whims: lack of adjustment

In today's materialistic world, couples are breaking off for reasons that were unheard of.

Rashmi, who looked very distressed during counseling, said "Never in my life, did I have breakfast without fruit juice. Madhav and his family members would take tea in breakfast. Anyway, I adjusted myself to their routine. Once I told Madhav that I can't have Chapati-Subzi in breakfast. Instead of appreciating that I was not used to their kind of breakfast, he indifferently told me that I should make my own breakfast, if I don't like what is cooked.... That was not all, Madhav made a big issue out of my mother's advise for healthy diet at least during pregnancy."

Madhav in a separate session, confided "Rashmi's mother interferes too much in our marital life. She keeps imparting instructions at every small little thing. He took out a piece of paper from his file, which read –

"Breakfast	:	5 almonds + 1 glass orange/ fruit juice + 2 eggs + Toast etc.
	:	Milk – one hour after breakfast
Lunch	:	2 Chapatis + 1 green vegetable + Paneer/ Chicken etc. + 1 katori dāl (lentil) + Curd
Evening Breakfast	:	1 glass milk + Snack-Poha/ Sandwitch etc.
Dinner	:	2 Chapatis + vegetable + dāl (lentils) + Curd + green salad
Before Sleep	:	One Glass milk"

Madhav told, "Rashmi's mother handed over this diet chart to me, when I went to her place to bring Rashmi back. Do I not love Rashmi? Do I not take care of her health and other needs? What was the need to humiliate me like this! In Rashmi's presence, her mother gave me sermons, "Rashmi may hesitate and may not be able to convey; that is why, I am telling you this. Please don't mind... There is no harm in taking her out at least on weekends, if you don't get time on weekdays. If sometimes you don't find time, you can send her to our house; she can accompany us on weekend outings.... Please don't mind... I, being her mother, had the duty to share Rashmi's difficulties with you."

"Couldn't Rashmi herself tell me her preferences for breakfast or lunch?"

Rashmi defended her mother, "My mother never interfered. This diet chart she gave, as I was pregnant at that time. She never suggested that I was not being properly fed by my in-laws. She gave it in good faith, out of her concern for my health; actually I wasn't gaining as much weight, as I should have, during my pregnancy."

Madhav butted in, "This is just one example of her mother's interference. She keeps phoning and imparting instructions to Rashmi at every step. I can't tolerate... It is so humiliating for me and my parents, she does not realise... When Rashmi doesn't trust me one bit, what is the point in living together.

... Her mother didn't spare even my mother. She called up to "request" my mother to see if something was wrong between me and Rashmi, "they haven't shared bed for last one week", she told my mother. How did Rashmi's mother come to know about that fact, if Rashmi was not sharing these personal details? Had she fit some hidden cameras in our bedroom? Rashmi was in the habit of keeping her parents posted of each and every happening at home. She doesn't feel ashamed in sharing with her mother every minor detail of our personal life and even what is happening in our bedroom each day. I am thoroughly fed up and can't take it anymore."

No amount of counselling could help. The only saving grace was that after contesting the divorce petition for about 2 years, Rashmi and Madhav agreed to part ways amicably and seek divorce by mutual consent.

Couples sometimes find it difficult to adjust to differences in each others' life style.

Different lifestyles- failed reconciliation

Saurabh had filed a petition for restitution of conjugal rights. Sheilley during in-camera proceedings was categorical that she was unable to adjust with Saurabh as there were serious irreconcilable differences between them. "He has problem with me on every small thing. He does not like my wearing western dresses; he does not stand my consuming liquor, even occasionally: he never accompanies me to any of my get-togethers. If I go alone, he screams at my returning late. Things reached nadir, when he cut my hugging trousers into two, as I challenged him that I shall wear what I like... when his own sister wears all kinds of dresses he doesn't mind."

Saurabh, shook his head and lamented, "Sheilley has no sense of dressing up for an occasion; she has no regards for elders and how to behave and dress, when they are around; despite knowing that my parents are orthodox and traditional, she would still go to wish them in her half nighty...... I have tried my level best to reason out, but no way; it's just not working ....But I can't let her spoil my three years old daughter....."

During separate sessions of counselling with both of them, it could be sensed that Sheilley was not ready to make any adjustments, so far as her life-style was concerned, even at the cost of her marriage, though she sounded concerned about her daughter's future.

Saurabh said he did not want to break the marriage, but at the same time, was firm that Sheilley should stop wearing her ultra-modern dresses. At least, when his parents were around; he did not even approve of Sheilley returning early morning after her late night parties. He wanted custody of their daughter, in case Sheilley had made up her mind to break the bond.

The conflict between Sheilley and Saurabh was very limited: basically confined to their life styles, but still too big to be resolved. Both said that they didn't want their marriage to break but at the same time, both were rigid; neither of the two wanted to find a golden mean.

Sheilley came from a family of Army Personnel and Saurabh from a traditional Kayastha middle class family. Being the only son of his parents, Saurabh always felt obliged to see that his parents were happy and everything happened with their approval. Sheilley did not see anything wrong with her life style.

You don't have to be a rocket scientist to understand why the relationship between husband-wife and between parents-in-law and daughter in law is like walking a tight rope without any balancing device; or like driving around an alien planet without a map. This is not the easiest relationship. But neither of the two was ready to appreciate this fact.

Counselling by the court proved futile, as both Sheilley and Saurabh refused to recognise that difference in their backgrounds was the root cause of differences in their perception. They could have attained convergence, had they made an effort with the goal that their marriage had to work. Little bit of adjustment by each side could have saved their marriage.

Swami Vivekananda said, though in a different context, that "we tend to reduce everyone to the limits of our own mental universe and begin privileging our own ethics, morality, sense of duty and even our sense of utility." This is so very true of any relationship including marriage.

In the context of religious conflicts, Vivekananda said, "All religious conflicts arose from this propensity to judge others. If we indeed must judge at all, then it must be according to that person's own ideal, and not by that of anyone else. It is important therefore, to learn to look at others through their own eyes and not to judge the customs and observances of other through the prisons of our own standards."

This applies no less to marital conflicts.

People have varied tastes and ideas and nobody can judge others whether they are right or wrong. The same thing may be perfectly all right for one person and wrong for another. Also, the same thing can be right in one moment for a person, and in another moment it can be wrong because the mind keeps changing constantly. We all carry a moral and social straight jacket which has been implanted in us for centuries. These categories of right and wrong are fictitious. Life is not divided into black and white. A lot of it is more like grey. Respecting each others' different ways would go a long way to attain harmony.

How can we forget that no two set ups have common trappings?

I Promise

I promise to give you the best of myself
and to ask of you no more than you can give.
I promise to respect you as your own person
and to realize that your interests, desires and needs
are no less important than my own.
I promise to share with you my time and my attention
and to bring joy, strength and imagination to our relationship.
I promise to keep myself open to you
to let you see through the window of my world into
my innermost fears and feelings, secrets and dreams.
I promise to grow along with you
to be willing to face changes in order to keep our relationship
alive and exciting.
I promise to love you in good times and bad,
with all I have to give and all I feel inside

in the only way I know how:
completely and forever.

Dorothy R. Colgane"

Privacy does matter

Savitri from a lower-middle class family, found her father-in-laws' preachings about keeping her undergarments clean and to change them after return from work, scandalous. "One fine evening, when I returned from work, I was shocked to see that my father-in-law had washed my stack of used undergarments. It was really too much. I had warned Naveen to tell his father to keep off my personal things," said Savitri.

Naveen was shocked at Savitri's reaction. He could not fathom as to what was so wrong with his father having cleaned her laundry.

Savitri actually missed the point that Naveen had lost his mother, when he was 2 years old. Naveen's father had brought up Naveen and his elder brother, who was just 5 years old at that time, single handedly. Naveen's father had been playing mother's role as well, while tending to both the sons. Naveen therefore, did not find anything odd in his father looking after his daughter-in-laws' affairs, in the same manner as he looked after their's. Naveen's father also did not realise that it will take Savitri sometime to adjust to their way of life, and to accept her father-in-law as her father or for that matter as her mother as well.

Savitri appeared to have developed an aversion towards Naveen's father on that count and other such matters; she felt that Naveen's father was taking "too much" interest in them. This became the bone of contention between Savitri and Naveen. Naveen shared that Savitri gave him an ultimatum, "You will have to choose between me and your father; either he will stay with you or I will". After pronouncing her verdict, Savitri did not even bat an eyelid before collecting her luggage and leaving for her parents' place...."

Naveen filed a suit for restitution of conjugal rights. During counselling, Savitri refused to relent. Naveen expressed his helplessness to leave his father, who single-handedly brought him up, making a lot of sacrifices.

Naveen's father, with folded hands pleaded that Savitri should return home and suggested that he shall construct a room on the terrace and shall shift there.

Savitri still could not make up her mind, as she felt that the very presence of Naveen's father in the same premises would be a constant source of bickering between them.

Getting into any relationship, including that of a man and wife, with the 'preamble' that "effort has to be made to make the relationship work," it will surely work.

If it fails in spite of the best of efforts, one would at least have the satisfaction that he/she has given it his/her best shot. This 'preamble' would strengthen one's tolerance to give an opportunity to the spouse to adjust to the new association; it would also help in accepting the fact that there is nothing like a 'perfect match" and that one has to find ways to make things look attractive and the bond beautiful.

You would realise that in your thoughtful journey, you are making the world a beautiful place for all, especially your next generation.

Accept the imperfections: Am I perfect? Ask yourself

One may not have a perfect marriage or a perfect spouse but accepting this fact brings contentment. Expecting and accepting imperfections bring peace. Conflicts exist in every marriage. Fighting fair and for the relationship and not just to win is healthy in marriage. Marriage needs tolerance, adjustments, communication, caring, nurturing, love, realistic expectations and a sense of humour to be successful. It is hard work indeed! But the returns of investment made in this relationship are immensely satisfying.

I myself came to find peace, on this reality sinking into me. Earlier, I would scream at the way my husband squeezed the toothpaste tube; left the tube uncapped; left his wet towel on the bed. He would get irritated by my sāree left unfolded all over the bed, and by my long phone calls and endless such events. He would be utterly mystified by the amount of talking I did with my female friends. Sometimes, when I would be on the phone, my husband would run an errand and upon his return would find me on the same call. "When I talk to my buddies, we stick to the specifics. But women take forever to get to the point. It's a total waste of time," he would say.

I would be unapologetic. "My connection to other women makes me feel good and be a better wife and mother." I would say.

With time, I realised that women get personal with other women as a way of understanding and coping with their experiences. They look to other women for help and reassurance. Women friends validate each other. But my husband did not get it: he would say "you are always hard pressed for time; you would have a lot more time if you were not on the phone so long!"

Men and women are different. Some of it is biological and some of it is how we socialised, but the result is the same. Instead of appreciating these distinctions, we often misunderstand each other.

Charles T. Hill, a Psychology professor says that men and women even get jealous over different things. A man tends to be jealous of potential sexual partners, while a woman tends to be jealous of time her husband spends away from her, whether it's with drinking buddies or just golfing. She wants to feel that she is No.1 in her partner's life. A husband may think "But she knows she's my top priority. Yet if I often work late or spend a lot of time at the gym, she doesn't know it." A wife views her marriage as a partnership but men's attitude often is that they are helping the wife out when they pitch in, like the dirty dishes etc. are just hers and not his as well.

Recognising these differences can alleviate confusion and hurt feelings.

Sooner than later, I discovered the fact that to expect two different personalities of different genders to live together under one roof without any clash is too much to expect. Dawning of the realisation that two views on each point would always be there, brought me peace. With time, I came to see these irritations as a part of living together. We have learned to laugh at each others' imperfections.

An actor/ director recently shared with a leading daily, "It is the equation between two people that sustains a marriage. And we treat each other as two different individuals, and not one entity called marriage. Her husband said, "It's good that none of us has tried to change the other to fit into a preconceived notion of a partner." She chipped in, “Well, he takes his own decisions and I take mine. We don’t decide for each other... We disagree all the time. I’d suspect couples who don’t argue and are always in agreement. We disagree over a lot of things. When, we’re watching the news, we end up with different political viewpoints, and that’s enough to argue the evening away[1].” Disagreements and differences between spouses would always be. It must be accepted and lived as a part of life. There is no “perfect match”. Your search for the “perfect match” will get you nothing but heartache and will lead you nowhere because two individuals, who come together with their own imperfections cannot be expected to create a relationship, which is perfect. Accepting this reality makes life easier.

> “I didn’t marry you because you were perfect. I did not even marry you because I loved you. I married because you gave me a promise. That promise made up for your faults. And the promise I gave you made up for mine. Two imperfect people get married and it was the promise that made the marriage. And when our children were growing up it wasn’t a house that protected them; and it wasn’t our love that protected them: it was that promise.”
>
> Thornton Wilder in play “The skin of our teeth”

Treasure good times

It is a myth that marriage makes people happy. Get out of it, the sooner the better. We can’t expect our spouse to be the sole source of our happiness. Our personal happiness must come from within. Marriage can complement our own individual happiness, but it cannot be the primary source.

The more you pursue happiness outside, the more it eludes. The trick lies in looking within for that elusive goal, rather than chase it around in your spouse and his folks.

Treasure exciting moments in the relationship as you never know when you may tumble down the hill. The treasured moments would be your saviour when you hit the rock bottom.

An apache blessing

Treat yourselves and each other with respect, and
remind yourselves often of what brought you together;
Give the highest priority to the tenderness,
gentleness and kindness that your connection deserves;
When frustration, difficulties and fear assail your
relationship, as they threaten all relationships
at one time or another,
remember to focus on what is right between you,
not only the part which seems wrong.
In this way, you can ride out the storms when
clouds hide the face of the sun in your lives –
remembering that even if you lose sight
of it for a moment, the sun is still there.
And if each of you takes responsibility for
the quality of your life together,
it will be marked by abundance and delight.
Love the one you are with.

—Unknown Poet

Petty matters are best ignored

We tend to focus on minute details and find fault with the smallest of issues. What we focus on grows. When we keep focusing on small weaknesses in someone, they continue to grow in our minds till we perceive them to be big problems in that person.

Would you want to live in a world where everyone looked, acted and thought exactly as you do? The world would be a pretty boring place in that case. To live a happier, more peaceful life, begin to see the unique qualities of your companion. Rather than criticising, appreciate and respect the distinct personality of your spouse.

Generally, we perceive in others the weaknesses that we need to address within ourselves. Let us stop blaming and condemning others. Working on changing ourselves and things we don't like about ourselves, before we change others, would bring immense peace and harmony. Efforts made for attaining a "perfect self" would help one to look for positive in others and in constantly working on one's own negatives.

Different ways : different values

Apurva Ghosh is a surgeon and Sonali, a software engineer. Apurva, the only son of his parents, was staying with his widow mother and married sister and her five years old son. Sonali's father, a Retired Gazetted Officer, suffered from chronic heart ailment. Sonali has two sisters and no brother.

Apurva and Sonali got married at the age of about 28-30 years; it was an arranged marriage. Happiness in their marriage lasted only for seven days of their honeymoon. On return from Shimla, both joined their respective duties. Sonali preferred not to wear jewellery to office except an imitation gold chain. Apurva's family did not like this. Sonali's justification that she did not want to take the risk, as she travelled by public transport did not go down well with Apurva's mother, a traditional and orthodox lady. Apurva's request to Sonali to wear it for his mother's sake was met with an argument that her father advised her against wearing gold while traveling by public transport, which added fuel to the fire.

A few days later, in response to Apurva's advise to take the bus from Mool Chand bus stop instead of Andrews Ganj bus stop, Sonali told him that her father advised her to take the bus from Andrews Ganj because the frequency of buses from that bus stop was better. This irritated Apurva no end. Although, till then there was no issue between them, but a point of friction arose that Sonali goes by whatever was told by her father. Apurva developed a 'not so happy' feeling about Sonali's father. He felt that Sonali's father was interfering in their personal affairs.

Hardly a week had gone by that, Apurva's mother called up Sonali's mother and told her, "You have not taught Sonali to cook. Sonali does not even know to prepare 'Macher Jhol' (fish curry); she only knows to cook rice and boiled potatoes". When Sonali came to know about the same, she lodged her protest with Apurva. Sonali was rather more hurt by Apurva's indifference, as Apurva simply chose to ignore her.

Then, the first Holi after their marriage arrived. Sonali's parents invited Apurva and his family members for the Holi Celebration. Apurva avoided the invitation, on the pretext that he had already committed to his friends, but generously told Sonali that she could go. Sonali did not like it, although she didn't say anything.

At the month's end, Apurva's mother made a query about Sonali's salary. Sonali told her that she was open to contribute to family's expenses and wanted to know the amount she should withdraw. This led to exchange of glances and some whispering between Apurva's mother and his sister. Perhaps, they were expecting that Sonali would hand over her entire salary. Apurva's mother later suggested that Sonali should open a "joint bank account" with Apurva, in a nearby bank. Sonali having seen her friend suffer on this account was hesitant initially, but then told that she would do that on her next "off" day. This hurt Apurva, as he felt that Sonali didn't trust him. Sonali also was embarrassed by this episode and thought, "Couldn't Apurva have discussed this money matter, in privacy? Couldn't have they sorted out modalities of sharing financial burden of the family, between two of them?" Insensitive handling of the entire issue not only hurt Sonali but also left her feeling insecure; she wondered, "Why so much emphasis on money matters, within hardly a month of their marriage." This insecurity added to Sonali's apprehension about opening a joint account with Apurva.

Sonali's insecurity can't be brushed aside lightly. There are numerous real life-stories of brides being robbed of their entire finances, made dependent upon husbands or in-laws, even for their day to day expenses. Sonali's initial hesitation and shying away from this arrangement did not necessarily reflect her distrust. It may be good to be forthright once, rather than repent later.

This issue could have been handled more wisely and in a tactful manner.

Soon another point of friction arose between them about Sonali visiting her ailing father every weekend. Sonali being the eldest child felt responsible and more so, as she was the one, who used to take care of her father's medicines and visits to the doctor, prior to her marriage. Apurva accompanied her once but later on started avoiding visiting his in-laws on one pretext or the other. Apurva's mother also did not like Sonali's weekly visits to her parents, as she felt, Sonali's parents instigated her.

Sonali's mother invited Apurva and his family members for "Jamāi Shasthi". Apurva's mother did not go; Apurva also agreed to visit his in-laws on that occasion with great reluctance. Sonali's mother-in-law later revealed that she did not go as Sonali's parents did not invite Apurva's sister properly. These instances coupled with some more such issues caused a rift between Sonali and Apurva.

The rift could not be wedged. Ultimately, Apurva decided to part ways and filed a petition for divorce on the ground of cruelty quoting all the above incidents in support. After marriage, Sonali and Apurva had effectively stayed together hardly for 2-3 months but contested the divorce petition for almost 10 years, ultimately Apurva losing the battle. Repeated efforts for reconciliation and counselling during the pendency of their divorce case did not bear any fruit. A patch up could not take place. Sonali did not agree for divorce by mutual consent as she felt that her life had been ruined by Apurva for no significant reason and for no fault of hers.

Life would be much easier if one could remember that one's spouse is a personality distinct from one's own, brought up in a manner and in an environment, different from one's own. The values imbibed by the spouse may be totally different from one's own.

There is no point getting too touchy about the advise given by one's spouse's parents, if it is innocuous and does not affect the relationship in any material way. Once mutual faith and confidence is built up, the spouse would stop looking outwards for guidance.

Demanding instant compliance to your ways: avoidable

The story of Sheena reaffirms the point that demanding instant compliance from the spouse to one's own way of life is surely avoidable.

Sheena, a well educated beautiful Bengali girl was married into an Army Personnels' family. Although Akash was not in forces but having been brought up in that kind of a disciplined atmosphere, was stickler of rules. Akash had filed a petition for restitution of conjugal rights pleading that there were hardly any differences between him and Sheena. There was no reason why Sheena should not join his company.

Sheena during 'in-camera' proceedings shared, "Things are small but unbearable. I cannot live under army rules. Akash is an egocentric person, who expects an impossibly rigid standard of behaviour from me. He is a stickler for domestic discipline and I can't live by the desired perfectionist code of conduct at home, in get-togethers: formal and informal. You can't imagine that he drew up a long list of do's and don'ts for me to follow. No sane person can be expected to live by that regimentation."

Sheena showed me a list of instructions given by Akash, to be adhered to by her. The same made an interesting reading:

"1. Not to put more than 3 tea spoons of milk in the tea;
2. Not to serve tea in wet cup;
3. Not to forget to put saucer under the cup, when tea is being served to the guests;
4. To change the hand towel, whenever wet;
5. To change the night dress, immediately after getting up in the morning...."

There were many more instructions like these; some were out and out hilarious. This reminded me of an old case of Dr. N.G. Dastane Vs Mrs. S. Dastane, where the husband had a still longer list of instructions to be complied with by the wife, which read:

1. On rising up in the morning, to look in the mirror,
2. Not to fill milk vessel or tea cup to the brim.
3. Not to serve meals in brass plates, cups and vessels.
4. To preserve carefully, the letters received and if addresses of anybody are given therein to note down the same in the note book of addresses.
5. After serving the first course during meals, not to repeatedly ask 'what do you want?', but to inform at the beginning of the

meals how much and which are the courses.

6. As far as possible, do not dip the fingers in any utensils.
7. Not to do any work with one hand.
8. Keep Chi. Shuba six feet away from the primus stove and Shegari.
9. To regularly apply to her 'Kajal' and give her tomato juice, Dodascolin etc, to make her do physical exercise, to take her for a walk and not to lose temper with her for a year.
10. To give him his musts and the things he requires, when he starts to go outside.
11. Not to talk much.
12. Not to finish work somehow or the other; for example, to write letters in good handwriting, to take a good paper, to write straight and legibly in a line.
13. Don't make exaggerations in letters.
14. Show imagination in every work.
15. Not to note down the milk purchased on the calendar."

Giving too much importance to petty matters may not help; expecting one's spouse to get accustomed to one's way of life and to one's way of dressing up too soon may prove disastrous. Give your spouse some time to know your ways and get adjusted; respect each other's likes and dislikes.

Appreciating things that please you in your partner, rather than brooding over what irritates you, paves the way for a smoother "living together" with one's partner.

Sharing love, sharing matter

Sharing a beautiful relationship with one's spouse does not necessarily mean sharing anything or everything, whether worthless or valuable in monetary terms. Loving each other does not presuppose an agreement to share all possessions unconditionally. We all have a child within us. A wretched soft pillow, which your wife brought with her might be worthless for you. But the same may be a prized possession for her. Kshama was used to a "Barbie Doll" soft pillow since her teenage; she carried the pillow to her matrimonial home after her marriage. Arun used to tease her about the same. So far so good, she did not mind.

One evening on her return from work Kshama found her "softy pillow" missing; she went berserk on finding Arun's nephew soiling it; she screamed and howled. Arun was thoroughly upset at Kshama's outburst. Both were angry and did not speak with each other. Not only that, even Kshama's mom-in-law was at a loss to understand all the hulla-baloo about that stupid pillow. They lost the point that a possession may be worthless in monetary terms but it may still be very precious for someone.

Money matters are sensitive. Not surprisingly money manages to create a wide wedge between many couples. Most people think that spouses break-up on the grounds of bad behaviour of the spouse, issues pertaining to children and the loyalty of the spouse etc. Money is not generally contemplated as a big issue, but money is also one of the factors in breaking up of marriages. Of course, not in India but in western countries, money is one of the major issues in a marriage.

Experts on psychology, divorce and finance say that before walking down the aisle, couples should have a talk about their financial health and goals.

Marrying a person who shares your attitude towards money might just be the smartest financial decision you will ever make. In fact, your marriage might prove to be your most valuable asset – or your biggest liability. Betsey Stevenson, Assistant Professor of Business and Public Policy at the University of Pennsylvania's Wharton School, who researches the economics of marriage and divorce says, "A lot of choices we make in how we want to live our lives involve how we spend our money."[2] When you share similar outlooks on money matters – or when you can, at the very least, find some middle path, it paves the way for preservation of your marital asset, your union.

Unfounded financial insecurity

If Sonali's case is the one end of the spectrum, at the other end of this spectrum is the case of Renuka and Rakesh. Renuka was a Class-II officer with Delhi Police and Rakesh, a practising lawyer.

Both were initially living in joint family in a bunglow owned by Rakesh's father. Renuka could not adjust with her in-laws. Rakesh, for the sake of mental peace decided to move out. The separate establishment brought with it, extra cost. The children needed to be kept in a crèche. Not only that in the joint family Rakesh never bothered to find how the family affairs were being run by his parents, except contributing a fixed sum. With the separation, he felt the crunch. When in the last week of a month, Rakesh told Renuka "I can't bear the burden of your trip to Haridwar and Rishikesh. You better travel later or you incur the expenses out of your own salary," he could hardly complete the sentence before all hell broke loose. Renuka retorted that she had already invested all her money in bonds and was hardly left with anything.

After sometime, Renuka and Rakesh decided to purchase a flat. Renuka's father visited the couple and advised Rakesh to book the flat in Renuka's name. Rakesh not only felt offended but was also deeply hurt at the "instructions" of Renuka's father. There was an argument between Renuka and Rakesh after Renuka's father left. Rakesh decided that he would not buy the flat at all. But keeping in mind the welfare of his daughters and to diffuse the tension at home, Rakesh applied for the flat in Renuka's name.

On another occasion both Renuka and Rakesh went to the market to purchase a bicycle for their elder daughter. The younger daughter also started crying for a bicycle. Rakesh was not carrying enough money to buy two bicycles. Although Renuka carried enough cash but she did not offer to contribute, despite the tantrums being thrown by the younger daughter. Neither did Rakesh ask her for money.

Having come to understand Renuka's financial insecurity, Rakesh ultimately stopped asking her for money or even for her salary's account. Since the time Rakesh decided that his priority was peace at home over money matters, everything is going fine. Rakesh confided "I was initially crossed with Renuka on this issue. We had major fights on such issues. But then I thought it was doing no good to our daughters. I could not even walk out of marriage for our daughter's sake. Having seen the fate of children of my uncle's broken family, I could not do that to my kids. I then asked myself, what did I actually want. I decided in favour of healthy and happy growth of my daughters in a peaceful atmosphere. That was the turning point in my life. That day I told myself that for me, Renuka's job and salary do not exist. ...that was the day, I bought peace for myself. Since then, I have never asked for a penny from Renuka. Nor have I shown any curiosity as to what she did with her earnings. We are having a good life since. No doubt, sometimes I do feel hard pressed financially. But then, I have learnt to run the household within my own means... Over a period of time, Renuka's attitude has also softened a bit."

Women since ages were conditioned to accept the man as the protector, provider and the care taker of the family. Perhaps, Renuka could not get out of it and thought it was Rakesh's duty to fulfill all their needs and her hard earned money was just hers.

Rakesh, I feel acted wise and did not precipitate the matter. Certain wise adjustments for peaceful co-existence are definitely required.

The choice to decide about our priorities is totally ours. How we want our relationship to progress is in our hands. Take a stand and then forget about the other's small follies, if you want the relationship to work.

Harmony at home brings peace and joy in society and harmony in universe. One can realise how important it is to make an association work.

Reflect before you snap

Take your time before you snap the relationship because you may not find that 'Perfect-tailor made match', you are looking for.

Take some more time before plunging into another relationship because the grass is not greener on the other side, as Rita found.

Mr. Malhotra, partially handicapped, lost his wife to a dreaded disease. Rita, friend of Mr. Malhotra's sister, was very sympathetic towards Mr. Malhotra. She encouraged Malhotra to involve himself in bringing up his children and helped him to get over the grief of loss of his spouse. Rita, who herself was going through a "bad phase" in her marriage found an outlet for her emotions in her sympathy towards Malhotra. This brought them closer. Rita after some time decided that she could not continue with her marriage and enough was enough! Malhotra's company gave her the courage to walk out of her marriage within a short span. She extended her helping hand to Malhotra and ultimately proposed to be Malhotra's life partner. For Malhotra, it was too early to get into another relationship but his family wanted him to settle down for the kids' sake. Finding a friend and understanding companion in Rita, he hesitatingly accepted the proposal and got married. Then started Rita's search for a "better" spouse in Malhotra; she started looking for qualities, which were disappointingly wanting in her ex-husband. As reality started settling in, in the form of Malhotra's handicap and responsibility towards Malhotra's children, friction started to develop; Rita's spirited beginning touched a low. She had a tough task convincing the children that she was their friend. On the other hand was the children's wary attitude and apprehensions, in accepting Rita, in place of their mother. Those ups and downs and efforts towards adjustments sapped Rita of all her energies; this reached a nadir, when Sweety, Malhotra's daughter screamed, while Rita was helping her in bathroom, "Papa, Mom is too harsh". Malhotra intervened, telling Rita to be a little soft while scrubbing Sweety. Rita fumed out of the bathroom, taking a wow not to help the children any more. This set the process of squabbles, ultimately leading to separation of Rita and Mr. Malhotra. Rita, more disappointed than what she was earlier with the imperfections of her ex-husband; Malhotra more shattered than he was with the loss of his first wife!

"People who leave a marriage for someone else often end up finding that person carried heavier baggage than the partner they left behind. Without the old, imperfect partner around to blame anymore we find it was our imperfect self that was the cause of our own pain all along....

... while the real guys we married may be flawed, at least they are people whose imperfections we are used to. At least they are men we can count on, men we loved once, may still love, and if we don't now, will love again. At least they are husbands who will stay home and baby-sit when we can't stand it anymore and need to run away from home for a few hours ......"

..... Iris Krasnow

It may be worthwhile to stick to a known devil than to opt for an unknown angel.

Leave the baggage behind

Not that the second marriage is an absolute no-no. Re-marriage may be a great opportunity for a happy new start provided one leaves behind the excess baggage of emotions from previous relationship. Rather, Feng Shui expert Gita Kapoor says that in a re-marriage, not only should emotional baggage be left behind but even the marital bed should be replaced. This piece of furniture holds the deepest and the most intimate energies. It can be difficult to find or maintain a new relationship in a bed that holds the energy of another person. If you can't afford to replace the bed, then at least replace the mattresses, beddings etc.

There are websites which help people unload the baggage of the past love by uploading it. Sites like www.ex-cessories.com and www.exboyfriendjewellery.com help estranged lovers and couples in disposal of small little sweet things of past.

These sites acknowledge that hidden deep in the recesses of armoires and tucked inside the velvet-lined drawers of jewellery boxes, everywhere are the flotsam and jetsam of relationships past, the usually well-intended gifts of watches, rings and bracelets, which one may want to oust from his/her life. Once the relationship is over, there is a dilemma how to get rid of these items which lingered for years.

Megahn Perry, 30, an actress and a writer and Perry's stepmother, Marie Perry, the founders of the site exboyfriendjewelry.com thought that a mix of cash and catharsis would be most satisfying. This site allows users to sell, auction, trade or simply give away the refuse of their amorous misadventures, but subject to a condition that they must tell the story behind every gift. The founders said that they intended this site to be more personal than other e-commerce sites.

These sites, thus provide a novel way of unloading disturbing emotions attached to one time treasure troves. One of the sellers, on this site described how she felt when she opened the diamond butterfly pendant that marked the beginning of the end of one relationship. "Butterflies in my stomach," she wrote. "That's what I had, when he gave me this." "Butterflies symbolise change, and he sure did," she added.

"I need it gone!" wrote one, whose sleek Gucci watch sold recently.

Others offered more details. "Reeree" wanted to unload a broken watch, the "Hers" half of a pair with faces showing the phases of the moon. "We had a thing for full moons," she wrote. She offered to give the watch away.[3]

Emotional baggage carried from the previous relationship can spoil the future. It is better left behind. Remove the traces of past from your life. Burying the hatchet is a sine-qua non for a healthy relationship. If one is getting into second alliance with the belief that it will bring stability in one's life, soul searching to find out what really went wrong the first time is a must. A divorced friend shared, "When I first got married I had this notion that marriage happens only once. But the break-up had put me on real ground. I have to be much more giving, much more forgiving; correct my own tantrums, weaknesses and limitations. I will take all the blame for my lost marriage."

If you have not understood the dynamics of what went wrong earlier and take responsibility of your part in it, you will carry a lot of unsorted stuff with you into your next relationship.

A second plunge and break up

Naman and Ritika were in court for seeking divorce for the second time. Both of them were divorcees, when they got married to each other. Their marriage lasted only 6 months. Naman complained that "she keeps comparing me with her ex-husband at every step. I even feel ashamed in telling that even sexual relations between us were not spared.... it was too much when she told me one night that Kartik enjoyed it more in a particular manner... I am fed up... I don't think she has got over and can ever get over her first relationship."

Ritika butted in "Only once did I make a mention of Kartik to him. He is exaggerating and imagining things."

No amount of counselling could persuade Naman. He was firm that he has decided to go it alone; he could not tolerate being compared all the time with somebody, even in love making.

The key is to resolve conflicts inside your mind and soul. Once your relationship is over, you should give yourself time and not immediately jump into another one. It is important to clear your mind and heart of all impurities that the last relationship has left.

Marriage entails a lot of issues and needs a lot of time and affection. If you don't understand this, it's all despair. More than what you want in a relationship, it's important to know what you don't want in a relationship. That will help make a second decision.

If children are also involved, it is very important to make sure that children don't feel the pain of your new partner. Their comfort level also needs to be measured and any dissensions need to be respected.

Recently, a celebrity re-joined her ex-husband. Today, the couple lives together for the sake of their daughter. She admitted, "Ultimately it depends on what your priorities are and the comfort level you share with your partner. For us, our daughter is our topmost concern. Since they share a very intimate relationship, I don't want to tamper with it. Also, I am happy with him around. And that is what matters.

... Of course, things would've been different had our daughter not been in the picture. Yes, then I'm not too sure, if I'd still be friends with him."

There are celebrity couples who have forgiven and moved on, like Suchitra and Shekhar Kapoor, Karishma Kapoor and Sanjay Kapur, Rishi and Neetu Kapoor; Sonu Nigam and Madhurima; Aditya Pancholi and Zareena. The bond of the couples who rejoined each other is probably stronger now, since there are no pretensions about it, no illusions about themselves, about each other or about their relationship. The second time round, it is a bond they have entered with eyes wide open, quite sure of where to draw the line; with minimal expectations and with a genuine desire to give the relationship a chance. This is quite in contrast to the first time, when one enters marital alliance riding cloud nine; high on expectations and ready to exit, in case things go wrong. When expectations are high, there is bound to be disappointment.

But everybody may not be as fortunate as these celebrity couples. Everyone may not get an opportunity to rethink, resolve and be together with one's ex-spouse.

Take your time, before you snap.

Give life a chance

You might have reached a point in your relationship where you ask yourself, "Why should I continue?" There are spouses, who moved on to be with someone else, believing him/ her to be more sensitive, loving, understanding and caring but had much graver problems than the ones with ex-spouses, leading to bigger disappointments. This experience not only made it much tougher for them to take a decision than the last time, but also eroded them of their self-confidence.

Sarita had approached the court for divorce the second time. Sarita and her first husband Vaibhav knew each other before marriage. Both were in the same college. Sarita had an affair with her class-mate Raman. But there was a break-up between the two over some triviality. Sarita became friendly with Vaibhav and his sympathy drew her close to him. By the time Sarita finished her graduation, Vaibhav proposed her. They married after going steady for about 3-4 years. Everything was going well, till an argument between the two, when Vaibhav taunted Sarita, ".... I should have known this. Raman must have left you for your wild temper. It was my mistake ...." That was it. Sarita was furious. That small remark became the turning point in their relationship. Any amount of apologising by Vaibhav did not work. Sarita was deeply hurt and could not get over that remark. Things were never the same. During counselling, Vaibhav had many grievances against Sarita, but he seemed genuinely apologetic to Sarita for his uncouth remark. Sarita shared ".... I cannot trust this man. Today he said this, tomorrow he may come out with more vulgar things...." Sarita did not feel secure in her relationship. She felt cheated; she also felt that the mutual trust between the two was now missing. Nothing could convince her to ignore that one off remark. Their relationship ultimately ended in a divorce by mutual consent.

As somebody beautifully put it, if you can fight with a sibling and get back together; revolt against your parents and be accepted back in the fold again; disagree with friends and then be reconciled, what's so unnatural about a reproach with your spouse? How many times siblings betray your faith? So, what's so much worse when you think your spouse has betrayed you? If the life you have shared with each other has been good and meaningful, why let one mistake wipe out that association? Wouldn't you give life another chance?

Sarika with Devesh

Sarika had made up her mind to remain single and enjoy her life. But that was not to be. Devesh was working in the same department of a leading private bank, in which Sarika was working. Some times, he used to drop Sarika home, on his way back. Sarika's father was attracted by Devesh's simplicity. He was anyway worried about Sarika, as he felt, he was aging and Sarika must get settled during his lifetime.

Sarika's father started pestering her to consider Devesh. Initially Sarika ignored her father's suggestion, but ultimately she gave in and agreed to marry Devesh.

Sarika's father broached the topic with Devesh. Devesh had no hassles with Sarika's "divorcee" status. Sarika's father's happiness knew no bounds. But Devesh's parents were not too happy with the alliance. Ultimately, Devesh's parents gave in and agreed.

Sarika and Devesh got married at a simple ceremony, in the presence of few close friends and relatives. Everything was going fine, till the day Devesh's mother asked Sarika to return home little early for preparing for "Karvā Chauth", the next day. Sarika expressed her inability on account of some official assignment. "For you, it may not be important. But it is Devesh's first marriage. We agreed to simple marriage, at your insistence. That does not mean, you will have your way all the time....." said Devesh's mother. Sarika left for office without saying anything. But she could not be at peace with herself throughout the day. She kept cursing herself for succumbing to her father's pressure. The more she thought about it, the more distraught, she was. She did not feel like returning home. She left office early and went to her friend's place.

Devesh reached home early as asked and was surprised not to see Sarika home. He knew that Sarika had left the office early. Devesh's mother narrated the incident of the morning to Devesh. Devesh waited for Sarika, who returned around 8 pm and went straight to her room. On Devesh's persuasion, she did accompany Devesh to the market, but her indifference was too evident. "Karvā Chauth" was over. But that bitterness lingered in Sarika's mind. She started comparing her association with Vaibhav to her present status in the joint family. She for a while, felt that if she had to adjust like this, she was better off with Vaibhav. Things were never the same. She lost interest in the relationship.

Apparently, there was nothing wrong between Sarika and Devesh, but the warmth of a husband-wife relationship had vanished. Sarika had lost confidence that she could pull on. Devesh had no option but to agree with Sarika to seek divorce, as he realised that their relationship was heading nowhere.

During counselling session, Sarika said that she had no complaints against Devesh at all; Devesh was also at a loss to understand and express as to what went so wrong; he could not give any reason for their break-up. Both said that they don't want to lose each other, as friends.

Sarika not only lost her relationship, but her confidence as well. She confided that she had developed insecurity and is not confident that she can be happy with anyone.

Breaking loose – no guarantee of bliss

Nobody realises that breaking loose does not mean getting happier. You never really know what's going on in another person's marriage or affair. You may not even know what really holds people together. The depth and complexity of this relationship can't be trivialised.

We tend to forget that there is no escape from our own imperfections, which are always with us. Adjustments with the 'other' would always have to be made because we carry our own baggage of imperfections. How can we have that the 'other' is a perfect match, when he or she also carries his/ her own burden of imperfections?

Marriage has great limits. Look closely at what you are leaving, before breaking up. Whether it is so bad that no dignified person can put up with? Whether what you are heading for is a better and warmer relationship? Take a closer look. On moving out, you may face the stark reality of dealing with ex-spouses, young kids between the two of you and also getting poorer after a divorce settlement. The Grind of reality may take the sizzle out of the libido.

"After ecstasy-the laundry" as the great Buddhist saying goes.

"Love is like fever which comes and goes quite independently of will," Stendhal writes in his book "Love". Understanding this frees you from looking towards someone else's relationship as a 'model' to which you may feel that your own marriage should measure up. No one reveals the complete truth. We will never know what is the cementing force between men and women? ...We don't see them in their bedroom. We can't understand why an outwardly horrid relationship lasts and lasts, and a nice looking relationship suddenly breaks up.

There is no one truth about any relationship, much less, the marriage.

You may be astonished to discover that the imperfect life and marriage you fled, is actually your sustenance.

Nina and Manuel

Nina and Manuel were happily married. But after some time, Nina started feeling that she has everything – a house, children, material comforts except the husband. She felt that the remoteness and self-centredness of Manuel was pulling them apart. Nina started complaining to Manuel about lack of his attention towards her and about not spending enough time with her and their kids. Manuel was going through a rough patch in his business. Initially, Manuel avoided Nina's pricks. But this only led to further nagging by Nina. Then, a downturn in their marriage began. Nina, instead of looking inward for answers, started searching for them, outside. She found that her friend Soumya was much happier with less comforts and money. Soumya and her husband Sunil went for movies almost every weekend; they hardly missed any exhibition in town; they would try every new restaurant, which was reviewed in the latest magazine. Nina's nagging became intense, sometimes quoting indifference towards her, and on other occasions, using children to blackmail Manuel. Manuel started avoiding returning home on time. He started looking for ways to be away longer. This in turn, led to an explosive situation at home. Ultimately, Nina found solace in an old college friend Amar, whom she bumped into at a Mall. She started sharing her grief with Amar. Steadily they drew closer. One day, Nina decided to walk out of her marriage. It was a bolt from the blue for Manuel. Amar had become friendly even with kids, so the kids also did not protest at staying with Amar.

A short while later, Nina found that though Amar was a good sport for sharing hobbies like watching movies, going shopping etc., but he totally lacked in sharing household responsibilities. With that, set in another disaster. Nina consciously or unconsciously started comparing Amar with Manuel, who at least made provision for all their needs. She had never felt any financial crunch before. The more she compared the two, the more uneasy she became in her relationship with Amar. Despite restraint, she blurted out her feelings. Bickering became more common between the two; the bliss was lost sooner than Nina realised.

Nina filed a petition for divorce, which shocked the life out of Amar. Amar was at a loss to understand Nina's insistence that she can't pull on with him. Amar, ultimately agreed for divorce by mutual consent. The kids were devastated, as they could not understand what went so wrong with their new fun loving papa.

The above real life story and many such similar stories reveal that no one can tell whether the extra marital affair one has fallen for, will be ultimately fulfilling. Exceptions would always be there. But, often you will hear that such affairs prove devastating.

Ephemeral romance

In an instant, I could feel that outwardly Ramā and Narender did not make a perfect match. Rama had fair complexion and was sharp and smart. Narender was wheatish, gentle and a simpleton. Interaction during counselling revealed that Narender didn't match Rama's smartness. It was Narender's suit for restitution of conjugal rights. During counselling, I could find out that Rama's only complaint against Narender was that, "He is so stupid that if his brother's kids come to stay with us, he would invite them to sleep in our bedroom. It is not that he is not caring; he is too simple to ever be romantic.... He would never notice my new dress or a sexy nighty, I would wear with a purpose... ." To me, Narender simply appeared to be too shy.

Rama's story revealed her yearning for a romantic spouse, which she could not find in Narender.

One needs to grow out of one's dream that marriage is designed to make one happy ever after. Marriage is a life situation, which forces you to grow into a responsible adult. The search for that fantastic man or woman with whom you will have never ending romance should be put aside after marriage, because that fantastic man or woman often exists only in your imagination.

Let us accept each other's imperfections.

The "perfect match" is a mirage. The day you come to accept this reality, your journey into the relationship called 'marriage' will take a higher plane in your own estimation. You would realise that your match may not be perfect but you can have a wonderful relationship – a perfect marriage.

For children's sake

If you break the family and walk out in the hope of settling with your new found love, the dark clouds may perpetually hang over your shining new love in the form of your children's sad faces, your parents' disappointment etc. Not many, who walked that path, have been hundred percent happy. It is very difficult to keep yourself happy when you hurt your loved ones. The pain one felt in marriage may be nothing compared to the pain one may feel once one is really cut off from the family.

Children deserve to be raised in a stable environment. It might be worth making adjustments and patching up differences by the spouses, in order to save the children from the trauma of emotional upheaval associated with break up.

A daughter's agony

Akshita's case revealed the stark reality of emotional turmoil which children of broken homes undergo.

Akshita was the 18 years old daughter of Usha and Naresh, who had been fighting a divorce case for last 13 years. Naresh had filed the petition of divorce on the grounds of cruelty and adultery. At the time of separation, their one year old son was taken away by Usha; Akshita, their four years old daughter, remained in the custody of Naresh. Akshita had joined her mother, about a month back.

It was hard to fathom, how a child who stayed with her father and grandparents for more than 10 years could happily join the mother after such a long gap. But separate session with Akshita gave it away. Interaction with her revealed the extent to which the children of estranged couples may suffer. Akshita's story could have easily moved anyone, even a stone-hearted person, to tears; it was heartrending. With a maturity of a young woman, Akshita shared,

"I was just 4-5 years old when my mom was turned out of home. I still remember my mom had severe headache that day; she could not cook dinner on time; but as soon as papa returned from office, she got up and started cooking. Papa was furious and screamed, 'Maharani, your resting time is not over yet. Why dinner was not kept ready?" I was standing with mom in the kitchen, when papa hit her from behind. I was too shocked to even cry. Not that I had not seen papa beating my mom earlier, but that day, it was too much. Papa pulled mom by her hair and threw her out of the kitchen; her head banged against the verandah wall. I don't remember what happened thereafter, as my grandma had taken me to her room.... I didn't find mom, the next day. Rahul, my baby brother was also missing. But I didn't dare ask papa about them.... With time I realised that mom won't return.

... Papa would pamper me sometimes and called me by my nick name "baby". He took good care of me. He even encouraged me to share with him anything and everything.... He married again... his wife was all right with me initially... then she had a baby boy... we named him Nikhil... I loved Nikhil and used to play with him... but you know what she did to me..." in between sobs Akshita told "his wife called me shameless when I told my papa about my periods... what was so wrong in it, I couldn't understand? Papa was the only person with whom I always shared everything, since my mom left. His wife even alleged that I have physical relations with my father. I was just 12 years old at that time... can you imagine what I felt like? I cried and cried the whole night. I could not eat or sleep ... But papa didn't say anything to her. I was deeply hurt and felt like seeing my mom. I kept telling papa that I wanted to meet my mom... but he kept on avoiding it... once he told me that it won't be good for me. The more he kept me away from my mom more desperate I got.... taunts of his wife made me miserable... I was missing my mom like hell.

... You know his wife would wash everyone's clothes but would leave mine in the corner of the bathroom, as if I suffered from some contagious disease... once I had severe stomachache and cramps during my periods and couldn't even wash my stained underwear; I had left it in the corner of the bathroom thinking that I would wash it later... I didn't even get up for dinner. Papa didn't even bother to find why am I not there for dinner... his indifference broke my heart. I was still lying in my bed with that unbearable pain, when his wife screamed from inside the bathroom... she came out of the bathroom hurling all kind of abuses at me... my stained underwear was hanging at the other end of the mopping rod she was holding. She paraded it in the entire house, and told my grandparents 'She has no shame. She is sprawling on the bed since afternoon. Couldn't she have cleaned it up?' I felt so ashamed... I wished I could die that very moment. I couldn't face anyone in the house. She made such a big tamāshā of the whole thing....

I was a brilliant student; I always stood 1st or 2nd till IX standard. I was very talkative and was popular amongst my classmates as well as teachers for my great sense of humour... But papa's indifference and such tamāshās at home gave me a lot of tension. I couldn't speak with anyone about the same. Every passing day, my yearning to meet my mom grew stronger. The more I wanted to meet my mom the more my father discouraged me... he didn't even give me her address or phone number... rather one day he got thoroughly irritated by my persistence and told me that I should forget my mother. She is a prostitute... You know he didn't use this word... he abused her in Hindi... I can't even utter that word.... I came to realise that I won't be allowed to meet her... I felt annihilated in the house... didn't know whom to trust and with whom to share my grief... I felt so unwanted and ridiculed all the time... I would hide myself in the bathroom and cry no end... I couldn't sleep despite efforts... tension and sleeplessness took its toll not only on my health but also on my studies... my performance started dwindling down.

Things came to such a pass that I stopped talking altogether; I had forgotten how to smile; I was not able to eat and couldn't even sleep for two days... ultimately I had to be put on sleeping pills. Nothing less than 3-4 pills worked. Even with 4 pills, I could hardly sleep for four hours maximum. My health started deteriorating. I slipped into depression. Ultimately, I had to be hospitalised... Doctor Uncle at LNJP Hospital, who was attending to me was very sweet... I confided in him that I wanted to meet my mom... my father was reluctant, despite doctor's advise...I hadn't eaten for three days and was on drip... Doctor Uncle warned papa that I may lose my speech if I didn't see my mom... Papa ultimately agreed to let my mom meet me... my mom visited me in hospital... I met her after about ten years... I didn't say anything but cried and cried... She started visiting me twice a week. ...Because of my hospitalisation, I had to miss my class X examination...

You know I wanted to be a doctor and was very good at biology; Mathematics was not my favourite subject... But Papa without asking me changed my stream to arts." She sobbed uncontrollably.

Catching her breath in between, she told, "... my papa has spoilt my life... he has spoilt my career... you tell me what would I do with arts?...I hate it... ultimately, I did my XII standard from open school."

"Did you have no good friends in school? Why did you not share your problems with any friend or her/ his parents?" I had asked.

You don't know Aunty! All my friends left me when my downfall in academics began... I don't blame them. Actually their mothers started "telling them to keep away from me... I have no grudge against them... who would allow their child to associate with a student like me, who was not doing well at studies. What to talk of my friends, when my own father called me "psycho". Do you know what psycho means? Do I look insane to you? Not once, number of times, he told me "You are turning insane and you will drive me also mad"... only because of such insensitive comments, I slipped into depression.

... You know I was never jealous of his wife, but she always complained to papa that I am jealous of her and also of Nikhil... You know I loved Nikhil so much... I always told everyone that we are two brothers and one sister. I always thought of Nikhil as part of our family....

Once I told papa that his wife scolded me for no reason; instead of paying any attention to what I was telling, he told me, "I had married her only after asking you. Now you can't blame me that I brought her to this house without your consent."

"You tell me Aunty! What would a child of 8 years of age know about second marriage or a step mother? I was just eight years old when papa had just casually asked me, "Akshita would you have any problem, if I bring another mom for you." I must have nodded. What kind of consent was that, you tell me? What consent could have I given for his remarriage, at the age of eight...? She asked me all of a sudden. "Do I sound weird aunty?"

One may find a companion along the way, after death of or separation from one's spouse. Remarriage may be a great option, no doubt. But the child may not take very kindly to it. Children may not accept your companion in place of a lost parent. Stories similar to that of Akshita revealed that constant friction between children and the second spouse may cause only rancour and unpleasantness; one may not get the peace and pleasure, which one might be looking forward to in the new relationship; one may end up doing the balancing act all the time, instead of enjoying the companionship of the spouse.

It may be wise to prepare the child and also to apprise the companion about ground realities before taking the plunge.

Male ego: The sense of possession

Let us be frank and admit that the empowerment of women at all levels has been so intimidating for men that they feel emasculated; they feel that they don't have the almighty position they held earlier. They were in total control and women were their possessions. Now they are companions. But how many men have come to accept that. Men are far more egoistic, and the reasons are obvious. For ages, wives have been conditioned to accept their subservient status in marriage. But not any more!! Women having acquired financial independence, refuse to accept that inferior status. Men, however, still continue to live in that age, because that is how they are brought up. Men have yet to come to terms with the role reversal. It will take some time before the male child is conditioned the new way.

The man-woman relationship therefore, is passing through a transitional phase. From sharing household responsibilities, to investment planning and sexual lives– both partners are equally involved. Most women now don't want to compromise on the quality of their lives or their sexual pleasures.

When both partners are working, both of them reach home almost at the same time. With disintegration of joint family, all household responsibilities fall on the couple. When they return from work, food is to be cooked and children are to be taken care of. If the children are left at a crèche, one of the spouses has to collect the kids while returning home. Unless both partners contribute, things will not work. Both are dead tired, by the time they hit the bed. This kind of marriage is an unnatural state for the man and the woman, conditioned differently since ages. Man was accustomed to being pampered when at home. He used to be tended to on his returning home. Children used to be asked to stop making noise on papa's return. That is how most of the men remember their fathers. But this may not be their reality anymore!

Give your man some time. Tell him politely but firmly, what you expect from him; make certain things clear before you give your consent for marriage. If you are serious about your job, make it clear that you have no plans to quit the job after marriage and even after birth of kids. There is no harm in sharing with your "would be husband" that you would expect his support to carry out your household and official responsibilities. Do not be afraid of losing a good match. If that is to be, then let it happen before marriage than after it.

Male ego is not confined to a particular community, caste, class or nation. It is universal. The other day, a national daily reported that successful young New York women were hiding their large incomes for fear of intimidating their potential boyfriends. It expressed concern, whether masculinity is so fragile that it can't handle being treated to dinner. Perhaps that is the reality.

A study[4] revealed that at least in five American cities, including New York, Boston and Chicago, women in their twenties are earning handsomely, more than their male counterparts. This revelation has touched a raw nerve among both sexes, as upwardly mobile urbanites struggle to adjust to a striking shift in the balance of domestic finance.

A query was found posted at some one's blog– Whether the male ego can cope with the potentially emasculating strain of being out-performed and out-spent by the new breed of fast-rising female lawyers, doctors and architects? It appears to be pretty difficult for men in their twenties to deal with "their hunter instincts"

Is it ok for women to pander to male insecurities by playing down their professional success, so as not to scare off potential husbands? A qualified woman electrical engineer from a reputed Engineering Institute shared, "When I tell a man what I do for a living, they get away so fast that they leave skid marks. I guess their dream is compromised by a woman who not only pays her own way but can also set up her own electronics."

Men have still to come to terms with women being all around, especially in the fields which were the exclusive domain of men.

If one of the spouses in a relationship is more powerful than the other or has access to more resources or money, the fear of loss and inferiority complex can set into the relationship. This translates into a relentless battle of power between the partners. If there is mutual respect, faith, tolerance and the will to keep it going, then nothing can beat this relationship. In life there may be some breaking points. But each time the relationship hits a roadblock and you repair it, it comes out stronger.

I Corinthian

Love is patient, love is kind
It does not envy, it does not boast, it is not proud.
It is not rude, it is not self-seeking,
it is not easily angered, it keeps no record of wrongs.
Love does not delight in evil but rejoices with the truth.
It always protects, always trusts, always hopes, always perseveres.
And now faith, hope and love abide, but the greatest of these is love.

—Unknown Poet"

***

- ♥ Beginning with the preamble that the marriage must work makes adjustment easier.
- ♥ Adjustment is necessary in every relationship, so is it in marriage;
- ♥ Accept the imperfections, because no one is perfect; nor are you.
- ♥ Search for a "perfect match" gets you nothing but heartache.
- ♥ Investments made in the relationship are immensely satisfying.
- ♥ Take your time before you snap.
- ♥ Second marriage is no guarantee of perpetual bliss, if you have not understood the dynamics of what went wrong earlier.
- ♥ If there are children, take your time in taking the second plunge.
- ♥ Having decided to settle again, bury the past; don't ever compare your spouse with your ex.

3

KEEPING MARRIAGE ALIVE: TILL DEATH DO US PART

A match may not be perfect, but the trends suggest that the older generations managed to survive the imperfections of each other. Whereas, now more and more people are walking out, and the reasons for the break-ups are as varied, as the couples themselves.

Today, everyone is talking about the quality of relationship. Spouses have become very demanding. There is no hesitation in quitting, if the partner does not come up to their expectations. Divorce has come to be accepted as a normal thing; Stigma attached to it has been diluted to a great extent. I have shared in this chapter some touching stories and the lessons I drew from them.

Dressing the wedding carriage: A day in life long marriage

Although in yesteryears, there was guidance given to Indian brides and to some extent to grooms also, to help in the transition to married life. With changing times, the relevance of such guidance is being questioned. Individualistic thinking, nuclear families and influence of all cultures around the globe has created a scenario, especially in urban societies where focus is now no longer on the contents of the letter but the envelope carrying it. Preparation with fanfare is made only for wedding and not for marriage.

Reasons for entering matrimony have undergone change. Salman Rushdie's recent statement that women wanted to get married because they wanted to wear a wedding dress, says it all.

Weddings are thought out in almost obsessive details. Designer invitations are sent along with exotic sweets or imported chocolates; much planning goes into selection of the bride's outfit and the colour combination to be worn by the bride and the groom; bride's accessories have to outdo those of cousins and friends, who got married recently. But hardly a thought is spared to this new relationship. Most people think that after marriage everything will fall into place and that they can simply sit back and enjoy the extravaganza. When there is hardly any preparedness to embrace the new role and set up, marriage exposes the couple to "marital shock", which sinks in once the celebratory period gets over.

To enter into marriage without knowing what it is actually about, is a great mistake. Like everything else, you have to work on your marriage to make it work. But, this aspect takes a back seat. The fact that pre-marital counselling is being talked about, shows that alarm bells are now ringing. In today's scenario, where there is a stark rise in percentage of marriages which are breaking up within first two years of marriage, premarital counselling assumes significance. Many people get into matrimony without having a clue about what marriage entails. The reality of living with another person in a new set up and dealing or adjusting with his/her way, and his/ her people's way of life, sinks in only a few months after marriage and then both the partners stop looking at each other through those romantic eyes. That ignorance, then usually leads to marital discord. One must realise that in marriages not only two persons but also two families (often two societies) come closer and get united.

Niharika caught unawares

Niharika was beauty personified. Anant was also handsome. Both belonged to rich industrialist families. Interaction with Niharika during counselling session, in Anant's petition for divorce, revealed that she had entered into matrimony without any idea about the marital relationship and the responsibilities it entails. She lived in her own world of fantasy. During counselling, she begged that she be given a chance, as she does not want her marriage to break. During a separate session with her, Niharika assured, "I am ready to adjust in every manner, I am ready to even clear the table after dinner. I have even started getting up early...." But at the same time, she had a complaint that "... despite my adjusting in every possible manner, I never hear a word of appreciation. Whereas, everyone in the family goes ga ga over Neeru, Anant's younger brother's wife because she is ready to lick their feet. Neeru will ask my mother-in-law every night if she should press her legs. I can't do all that drama...... You will laugh your heart out if you hear her English, particularly, the way she pronounces: "Valentines Day". She calls it "Valenteen Day". She lacks even social graces. Still, everyone is so pleased with her just because she is ready to act as a maid as well..... You know, at my parents' place I had never lifted my utensils from the dining table after meals, still I agreed to do so, as Anant told that everyone in their house did that. But, he never appreciated that ....."

On the other hand, Anant told that, "Niharika would keep sleeping till 10 am- 11am, absolutely unconcerned that I had to leave for the factory at 10:00 am; she would not even bother to join everyone for breakfast. Even after meals, she would simply rise from the table leaving the dishes behind, despite seeing that everyone else in the family kept their dishes in the kitchen. Not only this, on my politely requesting her to take care, she rudely told me that, "she has never done that. Servants used to lay and clear the table at her parents' house. She can't do the servant's job". This is not all. Once I had requested her to hire a taxi for going to her friends place, as her car had been taken by my bhabhi on account of some emergency. Niharika blasted me in front of the domestic help that she is not used to travelling in cheap taxis and ultimately cancelled her programme. .....It was the limit when, once, she all of a sudden started laughing at my pronunciation in front of my business partner. There are endless such incidents. I can't take it anymore. I can't allow her to humiliate me on every small matter. You know, she had once locked herself in the bedroom and had tried to slash her wrist, just because she had an argument with me on some issue. Enough is enough... How can I trust her any more. I will be in a soup, if she repeats something like that."

Despite sincere efforts and even intervention of parents and elders of the family from both the sides, Anant could not be persuaded to allow Niharika to return to the matrimonial home.

Niharika's case was an extreme example of the situation where a girl who was used to a secured, protected and luxurious life took a plunge into matrimonial alliance with great fanfare, having no idea at all of the demands of this all too delicate relationship. Marriage is not only the coming together of charming faces, dressing up nicely, speaking in impeccable English, enjoying physical proximity with the opposite sex. It is much more! Besides many other things, it is a relation that is expected to last till death.

Keep the flame alive: Let romance never die

Why does this association called "marriage", which commences with great excitement, declines at the same pace? What goes wrong? People forget that a good marriage does not just happen by itself. One has to constantly work on and invest in this relationship. It is a life time investment.

It is a myth that having married a person of one's choice, romance will remain alive for the rest of one's life. Nearly all relationships experience peaks and valleys. Everyday problems and challenges of married life can often cloud romantic feelings. This is when the decision to love is more important. A friend's father-in-law was suffering from Alzheimer's disease. He was not even able to recognise his wife Kaushalya, most of the times. But, Kaushalya's effort to take him out every evening for a stroll, lovingly holding his hand was admirable. She would say, "He has been a loving and caring companion for 40 years; now it's my turn to take charge of his health. Even now, my affection is always reciprocated, whenever familiarity is regained."

To have a lasting relationship, one has to forget that fairy tale of "living happily ever after". Relationships require maintenance. A good marriage does not just happen. It takes nurturing and work. While dealing with basic conflicts which arise in long term relationships, Stendhal in his book "Love" writes, "A man in love sees perfection in the object of his love, but his attention is still liable to wander after a time because one gets tired of anything uniform – even perfect happiness..."

It takes effort to keep monotony out of the relationship, to maintain its freshness and to keep the romance alive.

If you've been married for a really long time, marriage may get a little boring after a while. But it doesn't have to! There are small things you can do to make it a lot more exciting. We are too busy multitasking on multiple tracks. We seldom have "family time"; time, when all of us are together to chat, play, party or go for outing; that never gets on to our "things to do" list. Just spare a thought.

It is a common mistake that people make in thinking that just because they have married, they can sit back and everything will fall in place. They don't make the effort to share anytime together; they go back to long hours at work, taking the spouse for granted; they skip physical intimacy for months together, and then they complain that the romance has gone out of their marriage. A little bit of effort on both the sides can go a long way in keeping the relationship and interest alive:

A step, a twinkle in the eye
Hands that meet give much joy
Words of love rush into my heart
Kindling a flame; we can never part!

Conversation Essential: Silence Kills Relationship

Silence grows steadily between the partners, but this warning sign is often overlooked. In many long marriages, the desire to talk to one another vanishes, even as the willingness to listen diminishes.

Mary and John are middle-aged and have been married for 22 years. They describe their marriage as "good," although, they actually are just two people living side by side, rather than together.

"We both worked, then there were children and, either we had no time to talk or simply just didn't want to," recalls John. 'It's just the way we came to do things. It was always I, who brought up the fact that conflicts actually existed," told Mary.

"John was passive. Sometime along the way, I just gave up. But our silence became unbearable for me," Mary added. Mary had filed for decree of judicial separation. The couple was referred to professional counsellor. They had to relearn to communicate with each other. Meanwhile, their petition was kept pending.

Many couples think that the increasing silence between them is normal. It's as if to say, we've been married for more than 20 years. So, there's not much left to say to one another. Even I have difficulty in finding the time for conversation with my husband. But we know how important constant dialogue is. That's why we always take out time, whenever we feel something needs to be discussed. Most of the time, this works.

Men frequently tend to avoid conflicts. The general tendency amongst men is to wait and see if a problem just takes care of itself and goes away. They think, "If I ignore and don't deal with a problem, then it will just bounce away." It's better to face the situation and talk. We should realise when we are not together but only side by side. Good marriages are made of long silences and even longer conversations.

Green: Orange: Red: Sense the signals of gradual alienation

Kanak and Atul confided during counselling that they had been married for nine years, but neither of them could understand why, all of a sudden, they couldn't get along with one another. Increasingly, they started blaming each other for anything and everything.

Such accusations grew more frequent. "We have been together for nine years but it just isn't working out. I have been miserable with this person for the last two years," complained Kanak. It was during counselling sessions that they realised that their partnership hadn't got worse suddenly-but gradually.

It began quite innocently. Atul didn't have the time to kiss Kanak goodbye in the mornings, as he used to while leaving for work. Kanak was too busy in the evening to greet him, as earlier. Then, Atul stopped bringing home tit bits for Kanak, and she forgot to buy his favourite soap. "The little omissions added up," Atul recalled. "The distance between us grew also because we didn't talk about it."

"At some point, neither one of us was able to take the first step," added Kanak, "It became vicious."

"When he stopped bringing little surprises for me, it meant that I was not important to him anymore!" shared Kanak. Both became dissatisfied and waited for the other to initiate contact again.

This inner sense of alienation often shows up in the form of physical symptoms too. One partner starts suffering from stomachaches or headaches, sometimes both suffer at the same time. The distance between the two can become so great that they even deny each other sexually. It is then that one realises that something major is amiss.

Muddled head: Puzzled heart: Solemnly we drift apart

When both the spouses get busy in their own fields, they tend to look outward. If both are working, then it could be their respective work places. The toll of worldly responsibilities creates a lack of connect with one's better half. They drift apart.

Sunaina, who is working as an executive assistant in a large financial institution, met me after a gap of one year; there was a sea change in her personality. Instead of the usual grumbling about her husband Sunit not taking any interest in the activities she enjoyed, she seemed bubbly and lively. From her conversation, I could sense that she had started enjoying the company of Advait, a colleague of hers. A little more probing revealed that Sunaina's husband, being ever busy in pursuing his career, just had time for a routine conversation with her; that interaction was confined only to know about the well being of kids, buying grocery and other mundane things; Excitement in their relationship had disappeared. Although Sunaina loved him, she missed the attention she expected from him. "Attention deficiency" at home, led Sunaina to search for it outside, and the workplace was a convenient place to get attention and excitement.

Ira and Kamal – in the same boat

The story of Ira and Kamal was no different. Ira was a housewife and Kamal, a senior executive in a multi-national company. Initially, Ira was happy and remained busy with her kingdom and a new found authority to run the household single handedly. The arrival of a child kept her more than occupied. Kamal was also pleasantly poised in his career and its progression. But soon, the monotony of her life began to tire Ira. She started demanding more of Kamal's time and attention. Kamal could not understand Ira's sudden attention hunger. He felt that Ira had all the material comforts, then why a hue and cry all of a sudden? Kamal missed the point and could not see beyond the gadgets and comforts that he provided to Ira. Ira started withdrawing into a shell. The tension between Kamal & Ira drove Ira out of her matrimonial home.

Kamal filed a petition for restitution of conjugal rights. Kamal insisted that Ira had no reason to leave him; she had everything- a beautiful house, chauffeur driven car for herself, all the gadgets for her comfort and entertainment. Kamal could not realise that Ira missed his company. Ira and Kamal were fortunate, as Ira agreed to join Kamal on his undertaking to spend weekends at home instead of office.

An intelligent marriage is one that keeps evolving and adapting to changes with ease; a marriage needs investment of time to keep the romance alive. Keeping communication lines open helps one to sense the undercurrents; otherwise, both can be drifting towards different shores without even realising it.

Wording the unsaid: Communicate

Initially in my marriage, when hurt, I used to withdraw into a cocoon expecting my husband to know what had hurt me. I would sulk for days. With time, I discovered that I was hurting no one else but myself. Not only did such hurt and anger harm me emotionally and physically, but it also spoiled the family atmosphere.

It is natural to have disagreements. Rather, it is unnatural to be in perfect harmony all the time. It is quite normal to have arguments- it is better to say it all than suppress. Once you have thrashed the issue, then put it behind you. Do not rake up that issue again, when you are angry on some other count.

Communication between partners is the key to a happy marriage.

Once, a couple was celebrating the golden jubilee of their marriage. Many younger couples were eager to know the secret of such a successful married life. The husband told and the wife confirmed that at a very early stage of their marriage whenever they discussed something, it used to result either in sarcastic remarks or in a fight. So they decided to make a note of the mistakes of each other and discuss them on Sundays at leisure. They were mentally ready for something awkward to come from the other side. But soon they realised that they forgot many trivial things and slowly such issues were drastically reduced. This helped. The problems were not allowed to settle in their hearts and to hurt their relationship.

Expecting your spouse to know everything– what you need or what has hurt you, without you expressing it, is a little too much. Just because your spouse has married you, does not mean that he or she can read your mind. We have to tell our spouses, what our needs are, what our expectations are!

Say it!

Sumit and Nayantara have full-time jobs and they share the housework. Nayantara was entrusted with a special project, which was to take up more time than she had expected initially. Since the commencement of the project, Nayantara would return home very late and totally exhausted, "Why doesn't Sumit now take on more responsibilities?" - she wondered, as the housework piled up. "He's just making himself comfortable, while I slave in the kitchen. He must realise that I am more tired than him!'

But Sumit didn't notice a thing. It only struck him that his wife was becoming increasingly aggressive, exploding over every little thing. Sumit rather felt that he was being treated unfairly. After a bad argument Nayantara burst out, "Don't you see that I need your help? I can't do it all alone!"

"Why didn't you ever say anything?" replied Sumit, quite irritated. Soon, one thing led to another. Mutual accusations escalated and neither of them understood the other. Finally, Nayantara talked about divorce.

Only after they visited a counsellor did they begin to see reason again. They learnt to verbally express mutual expectations.

Men complain, "If she wants me to get something in particular for her birthday, why doesn't she tell me? Whereas, she thinks, "If I have to tell you, I feel diminished as a woman because it means that you haven't thought about me at all."

Many studies have confirmed that men and women think differently in a particular situation. It therefore, becomes all the more necessary for each spouse to verbalise his/ her expectations from the other. Beth Levine in "Secrets about Women, Husbands Should Know"[1] has narrated many such secrets revealed to her during her interactions with spouses. She narrates, "Paul Sabbah said "I have no answer when she asks – "do these jeans make me look fat?" He said, "If I say yes, I'm a dead man. If I say no, she tells me I'm lying. There's clearly no right answer." Wife Jennifer says, 'I want him to tell me I don't look fat, of course, but half the time, he isn't even looking at me when he answers. I guess, I'm just looking for reassurance that he still finds me attractive."

"When women ask for feedback on their appearance, they are really saying, I feel vulnerable. You have to do whatever it takes to make a connection, make me feel loved and secure," says Dr. Samuel Shem, a psychiatrist. "The right response is not yes or no, it's to make contact." Samuel says he and his wife have turned the question into a private joke. " When Narona asks if she looks fat, I answer, No, but do I look bald? Then she'll laugh and say no. We both know the truth; I'm balding, and she's not slim. But we also know it doesn't matter, because we love each other like crazy."

There are many things on which men and women may not agree conceptually. Books on the difference between men and women have turned bestsellers – "Men Are From Mars and Women Are From Venus"- by John Gray and "Why Men don't listen and women can't read maps" & "Why Men lie and Women cry" by Allan and Barbara Pease.

The magic of hug

Open display of affection, especially between couples, is frowned upon in India. When did you last hold your spouse's hand? When did you last hug him or her? We are conditioned not to openly express our affection. Even as mothers, we stop hugging and kissing our children, beyond an age. Hug someone you love! See how you feel!

It works wonders. Why is that skin-to-skin sensation so powerful? A touch goes beyond the physical and forges a connection that is more on an emotional level. Scientists say that gentle stroking activates the pleasure nerves beneath the skin, which then reduce the sensation of pain from the other nerves. Recent research has found that people who were exposed to painful temperatures on the surface of their skin felt less pain if they were stroked at the same time. The scientists believe that signals to the brain from the nerves that detect the pleasurable stroking dampen the signals from nerves that detect the pain. A neuroscientist has even calculated the optimum way of touching someone to produce the highest pleasure. It is believed that touch is crucial for children as they develop. Insufficient physical contact, while growing up could be implicated in the risk of depression in children, in later life.

There is even a branch of alternative medicine of healing by touch, in which one transmits positive energy to the diseased part of the body. Touch is a great way of communicating.[2]

If you observe closely, you will realise that the sensation of touch connects one better to the rest of the world than other senses. Children instinctively seek physical contact when happy or sulking. We become too conscious about our physical beings as we grow. We feel embarrassed at touching and hugging.[3]

The fact that Ma Amritanandamayi blesses everyone with her bear hug, speaks volumes about this gesture. Research has revealed that hugging releases the harmone oxytocin, which arouses a caring response in men and women. It creates a feeling of serenity. Hugging is healthy. It helps the body's immune system; it reduces stress, it is invigorating, it is rejuvenating and is nothing less than a miracle drug. It kindles warmth and affection, which is missing in day to day life.

Whenever one of us is home, it is understood that when the other leaves for work, he will give a quick peck to the other. Try doing it once in a while. You will surely feel more connected to your spouse emotionally. Hug your spouse when you find it hard to say sorry about something. You will realise that this one touch, has said it all for you. That's the magic of touch or of a hug.

Small gestures count

Hate is a short and sharp word that cuts to the heart and inflicts the wound deeply. Language is not significant, the meaning and the attitude cuts, and cuts sharp. Most often, even time fails to heal the wound and erase the scar.

Why use that 'hate' word when the small sweet word "love" can floor the spouse.

Forget grand gestures. Think sweet little personal things, which are the key to close and warm relationship. It does not require moving mountains. We learnt in the childhood– listen, don't interrupt; say "please," "thank you" and "I'm sorry". These rules apply equally well to marital relationship. It's so easy to let go of good manners. Try saying sorry, when you are wrong. Thank, when your spouse helps you in distress, and see the magic these words cast. These words help you to show to your spouse that you care and respect him/her. Dropping impolite habits also go a long way in avoiding bitterness. When you are really angry, give a sharp look, it would say it all without your uttering a word. Looks are more explicit. A friend shared, "When my husband was terribly late for an evening show, instead of creating a scene, I just told him "I understand you must have tried your best… I share your frustration. It not only relieved him of the burden of explaining but also created a lot of warmth and gratitude for me in his heart." It gave a feeling of oneness and of standing by each other.

Neeta, an old acquaintance shared, "Raman's habit of shrugging shoulders, particularly, in response to any desperate query of mine, irritates me no ends. Raman detests my shaking of head whenever he looks around for his misplaced car keys.....Once this small thing snowballed into a big issue between us. We then agreed to drop our irritating habits. I promised never to shake my head again at Raman. Raman agreed not to shrug shoulders. Dropping these impolite habits has made us realise that it was really rude to behave that way. Now, it's pretty easy for us to handle these situations without turning them into nasty fights."

Let compliments fly

'Try praising your wife, even if it does frighten her at first'.

- Billy Sunday

Don't keep nice thoughts to yourself. Even small compliments make big difference. When I tell my husband that "this colour combination looks great on him or that today he is dressed to kill. What is the matter?" his face lights up and he smiles from ear to ear. Seeing him bright, makes my day too.

Why are compliments so important? Craving for feedback is a basic human nature. We all want to know, how we look; how are we perceived. We all look for reassurance from the persons whose opinion we value most. A reminder that we are smart, good looking or kind, make us feel nice and fills us with zest to live up to our reputation, and up to the expectations of others .

My friend's husband would instantly light up, whenever she would narrate in his presence, that she was floored at the first sight by his Shahrukh Khan smile.

Genuine appreciation can bring an instant smile. Try it with your spouse.

Pleasant surprises

A neighbour who shares a great relationship with her husband, told "My husband will sometimes drop into my office for lunch because he knew I love being whisked away from work". Other friend, who is now happily married for a quarter century, told with great pride that, sometimes on returning home, she would find a hurriedly scribbled note on her table: 'Don't forget to take your evening dose". She would be touched that he really cared.

On an occasion she found a Vaseline jar on her bed side table, which she desperately needed on the onset of winters, which her husband must have seen on her "to-do" list and brought it for her. Such a surprise favour really touched her deeply.

It's hard, of course, to do these sweet little things when both the working spouses are deeply engrossed in their daily routine and tiring jobs; and both need and expect love and care from the other. But that's when a nice act has the ripple effect.

Experience tells that couples who share great relationships are not necessarily the smartest ones but are those, who have come to appreciate each other's best qualities and are kind to each other. Secret of their closeness is not scintillating conversation or fantastic sex - though they may have these in common as well. Their secret is that they've found out how to be kind to each other .

Kindness, tenderness, thoughtfulness, all these are greatly underrated qualities. We forget that it's the little moments of reaching out to each other that keep couples in love over the time.

What the successful couples understand is there's a karma to kindness: one small sweet gesture inspires reciprocal acts of goodwill.

We're all kind to our spouses. But its expression is lost in the humdrum of daily life. The happiest couples manage to show it effortlessly and frequently. They have turned it into their second nature. They can do it, even when they are bogged down by work and are chasing dead lines. Our acts of care and compassion also save us from self absorption and holding others responsible for our sufferings.

Respect feelings: Fix the Crack in Marriage Ceiling

Cracks can develop anywhere and anytime, more so in the newly laid ceiling of married life. A stitch in time saves nine.

Rakshandha and Arin belonged to the upper strata of society. Rakshandha was a beautiful, well-educated and pleasant mannered girl. Arin was equally handsome and well established in life. Arin was a senior vice president with the Indian arm of a British company. Rakshandha was working with an NGO. Arin was not ready for a child yet and Rakshandha agreed to wait for a year before planning a baby. A year went by, but Arin was getting busier with every passing day. Rakshandha did not complain when Arin could not find time for family get-togethers. She was fine even when Arin could spare only two-three hours for her sister's wedding. Rakshandha understood and appreciated Arin's involvement in his work.

After about 3 years of marriage, Rakshandha felt that something was missing in her life, but could not really pin point what it was. Rakshandha's sister delivered a baby boy within a year of getting married. This was when, Rakshandha realised that her biological clock was ticking and she also wanted a baby. She broached the topic with Arin. Arin hugged her and told her, "You are my baby. Why do you want another one?" But when Rakshandha insisted that she could not let her life wait for that beautiful event any more as she terribly missed the motherhood and wanted a baby at all costs, Arin refused in a very business-like manner, saying that he was in the offing to be considered for the president's post and was not in the frame of mind to take on the baby's responsibility at that juncture. Rakshandha again gave in, not wanting to precipitate the matter any further, even though she was not happy about it.

Another year passed by. Arin was on a constant rise in his professional life. He was enjoying his professional success and was basking in its glory, without sensing Rakshandha's pain. Arin kept on postponing the baby. Rakshandha on the other hand, started getting desperate for a child. One night, Rakshandha again tried to make it clear to Arin that she could not wait any more, but to no avail. Arin's total involvement in his job and absolute indifference towards her emotions and desire, led to alienation between the two.

Arin started avoiding getting into any conversation with Rakshandha beyond his mundane needs, dreading that she may not broach that 'baby' topic. Rakshandha had also given up on this issue.

One fine morning, Rakshandha came across a story in the newspaper narrating how artificial insemination brought smiles to a distraught mother, whose husband suffered from low sperm count. The story shook Rakshandha. It offered a way out, a solution to her desperation for a baby. Rakshandha visited Sri Ram Bharatia Institute, the same day to find, if she could be impregnated by artificial insemination. Very soon, Rakshandha went ahead with artificial insemination, and was happily pregnant. Throughout the procedure, she never thought about consulting her husband. "I did not find any need to share this fact with Arin, as he never understood my emotional need to bear a baby ... in fact he had no time to think beyond himself and his own job ..."

Three or four months later, Arin came to know about the pregnancy, when Rakshanda could no longer keep it to herself. Arin was stunned, and there was a major showdown between the two of them. Arin was so shocked and angry at the appearance of an unwanted baby, which was not even his own, that he just refused to accept the child. Rakshanda was equally adamant, and firm about having her baby. Eventually, they agreed to file for divorce with mutual consent.

No amount of counselling worked with Arin and Rakshandha. Arin thought that a baby had been delayed with the consent of both of them. Rakshandha felt that despite her adjustment with Arin in every possible manner, she was denied the joy of having a baby; Arin never cared to even acknowledge her emotions and emotional needs.

Rakshandha felt that she had done no wrong. She said, "I was undergoing an emotional upheaval; I used to remain depressed for no obvious reason; that is when I realised that my unfulfilled desire to have a baby and Arin's total indifference in this regard, was taking a toll on my health. Then, I took charge of my life and decided to go in for artificial insemination. You tell me what was wrong in it? ...."

Arin could not understand the intensity of Rakshandha's desperation. He felt that Rakshandha knew him and his desire to reach the top of his company and that she also understood his constraints; Arin was aggrieved that Rakshanda failed to appreciate that he was not in a position to take any further responsibility besides his professional calling, at that juncture.

Rakshandha and Arin looked like an ideal couple: good looking, well behaved, cultured, courteous and considerate towards each other. Still their marriage failed, because Arin refused to acknowledge Rakshandha's biological and emotional need to bear a child. Arin could not bring himself to accept the child Rakshandha was to deliver in a month or so. Rakshandha was also firm that she could not give away her baby. The differences between them could not be resolved, and they ultimately parted ways by seeking divorce by mutual consent.

An emotion of your spouse may be absolutely beyond your comprehension, but it has to be respected.

As We Renew our Vows

Today, we reaffirm our commitment to each other
as beloveds and partners in marriage.
We continue to strive to be sensitive to each other's needs.
To be open and understanding with each other
and to share our thoughts, our feelings
and our experiences with each other.
We renew our promise to try always to
bring out the qualities of forgiveness, compassion,
and integrity in ourselves and in each other.
We continue to cherish each other's uniqueness.
We continue to share in life's joys and remain steadfast
and comfort each other through life's sorrows.

—Unknown Poet

Rediscover your spouse: Explore the inner world

Many of us don't know what pleases our spouse the most. There is no harm in expressing what pleases you the most. "I know she loves roses. Once in a while I pick up roses on my way back home. The radiant smile Gunjan gives on seeing roses makes my day," said Vipin.

Finding out what pleases your spouse and doing that once in a while can keep your relationship fresh and fragrant.

Till one or two years of marriage love may be enough to sustain it. But thereafter, the relationship has to be nurtured emotionally and spiritually; one has to be intrigued. A staleness may settle in the relationship if the intrigue and interest run out.

How many of us talk to our spouses beyond matters of daily routine? In the humdrum of our existence, we are hardly left with any time to think with curiosity about our spouse. The hectic pace of modern life has also denuded us of our patience to observe and know as to what is going on inside our spouse.

A good marriage calls for maintaining freshness in the relationship. Both have to make each other feel important, which requires the spouses to remember and retain in mind, the partner's likes and dislikes, his/ her fantasies, career wishes and lifestyle.

No doubt, to be interested in each other takes hard work, a great deal of time and patience. But it's worth it.

Staying curious about the partner's inner world can keep the relationship alive and keep dullness from settling in. By nature, everyone would be willing to talk about themselves. In fact, most people never get a chance to talk about themselves and would happily do so, provided the person asking questions is pleasant and is genuinely interested in knowing about him or her.

Not only talking to the spouse but its timing is also equally important; to know, when to speak, and when to just let things be. A friend shared, "my husband is extremely cheerful and receptive in the morning. If I have to seek his advice on any matter or has to share something of significance, I do that during morning walks. Evenings are now meant for light talk, listening to him narrating about his day at office. I have stopped discussing such matters with him in the evenings, lest I am disappointed. This has worked quite well for me."

To keep a marriage vibrant, one has to swim with the tide and manoeuvre around the obstacles. Moods don't remain the same all the time. You can pick the times which are more conducive for showing interest or concern, and other times may be good enough just for routine talk.

Battle for equality: Both are right: Say no to fight

Sahil and Suzanne worked full-time till Leena was born. They had agreed before marriage that Suzanne would take a break from her job on arrival of the baby. The commitment was honored. Sahil meanwhile progressed well in his career. Suzanne soon found herself performing only the role of mother rather than that of a partner in bringing up the child. She shared this with Sahil. "Of course, it was clear that Suzanne could work again whenever she wanted to," he recalled. "But it was equally clear to me that she would still take care of the baby and the household as before." Suzanne on the other hand said, "I was financially dependent on Sahil, after I took the sabbatical. And he let me know it, too. I then picked up a part-time job, but I felt even more disadvantaged than before. I had two fronts to take care of."

Suzanne felt alienated in the relationship. Sahil felt that Suzanne had changed and had turned away from him. Both of them realised the strain in their relationship. Not wanting to risk destroying their relationship, they visited a marriage counsellor. During counselling, they realised that Suzanne was overburdened; she needed to work for self actualisation, but at the same time she also needed some leisure time; they agreed to employ a housekeeper for half a day, and Sahil agreed to spend a little more time taking care of Leena.

Equality in a relationship is not a static condition; it keeps changing with different stages in life. It is a matter of give-and-take for both partners, throughout. This giving and taking has often to be defined anew with every new life situation. In life, some 'my' moments are as crucial as "togetherness".

Lack of personal development – May prove fatal

There's always a danger of losing oneself in the relationship– through one's job, through kids, or many other such things. We have to guard against it time and again .

The first phase of marriage involves partnership building. During this, the partners are busy with each other and are generally close. But afterwards, they can drift apart. The decisive factor is usually the birth of the first child. If during this phase the woman feels neglected in her role as mother, it can lead to problems.

The next phase begins when the child starts going to school. Often, the wife then resumes working. Responsibilities have to be reorganised now.

The third phase starts, once the children have left home. Partners then have to get used to being alone again. Initially they may feel relaxed and liberated having discharged their responsibilities; this is treated as an opportunity to catch up on time to be with oneself and to be with one's partner. But this phase isn't easy. Often new power struggle arises; especially when one's professional life is over. It becomes difficult then, if either of the partners has not developed any personal interests over the years.[4]

"For at least a hundred thousand years, men have risen in the morning and gone out to find food for their families. Then the twentieth century brought an even bigger blow for men : retirement. Not only were they no longer required to hit a moving target , they were not wanted for anything. And herein lies the problem for the modern retired man. He still has a highly configured hunting brain that is literally unemployed. He's all dressed up with nowhere to go. Not only that, he's sitting on a remote beach where no one knows him or even cares about him.... Coping with a retired man in her life is often one of the biggest problems a woman faces. It can cause arguments, tears and even separation. He always seems to be 'under her feet', and may even start trying to take charge of her life, treating her as he may have once treated his employees, offering her solutions and advice when she really doesn't want them. And, frequently, he blames her for his own misery. ... A man's loss of identity is, in many ways, similar to the death of a loved one. They begin with denial, followed by depression, anger and hopefully, eventually acceptance.... Female partners can resent what they feel is an intrusion into what they see as a happy, orderly life. They may see their husband, for the first time in their lives, for breakfast, lunch and dinner. They can see he has so much free time – but he still never offers to help with the housework. Steadily, resentment and anger, can grow. As this rises to the surface, the man begins to feel rejected, misunderstood and worthless. When things get really bad, separation, divorce, and even suicide are possibilities."[5]

A newspaper[6] recently reported that in Japan, retirement has become a risky business for many wives, who are finding the stress of their husband's presence at home unendurable. Though after-retirement stress is a common problem in most developed countries, as husbands and wives try to balance relationships in their twilight years, analysts say Japan has become extraordinary for myriad reasons including the fact that one-fifth of Japanese are now over 65, the highest percentage in the world.

Sakura Terakawa, 63, a Japanese wife, described her four decades of married life in a small urban apartment as a gradual transition from wife to mother to servant. Communication with her husband started with love letters and wooing words. She said when her husband announced that he was ready to retire, she shuddered at the thought of having him around the house all the time. She said that was more than she could possibly bear.

Feeling chained to the tradition of older women remaining utterly dedicated to their husbands' well-being, Terakawa said, she devoted herself to her spouse. Retirement cut him off from his longtime office social network, leaving him virtually friendless and her with the strain of filling his empty time. She said that within a few weeks he was hardly leaving the house and was watching television and reading the newspaper and barking orders at her. He often forbade her to go out with her friends. "When he did let her go," Terakawa said, "she had to prepare all his meals before leaving".

After several months, Terakawa developed stomach ulcers, her speech began to slur and rashes broke out around her eyes. When doctors discovered polyps in her throat but could find no medical reason for her sudden burst of ailments, she was referred to a psychiatrist who diagnosed the stress as "Retired Husband Syndrome" - RHS. She began receiving therapy from one of Japan's leading RHS experts. She was advised to spend, as much time as possible, away from her husband.

To avoid an extreme situation like the one Sakura Terakawa found herself in, a woman needs to spare some time for pursuing her own interests and hobbies and make it known to the man; however, it surely also needs some skill to manage that hunter, the man.

To sustain a long-term partnership, one needs to keep reinventing oneself; one can learn new things or can even revive childhood interests and hobbies, which could not be pursued earlier for the lack of time. It not only gives a sense of purpose in life, but also enhances one's self-esteem. Your talent may even surprise your partner and get translated into heightened respect for you. It may keep your marriage interesting. It is a good idea to develop common interests, which may ensure some time together; and also to pursue one's own hobbies, to be with oneself and away from the spouse.

Besides dealing with and managing each other, life may throw up a situation where one might have to manage that "other" in one's life.

Extra marital flings

Our lifestyles have changed. One might meet a horde of potential mates at the workplace. With the increased working hours, interaction between opposite sexes at the workplace has increased manifold. Less time is spent with the spouse. One may find someone who makes one feel special. The temptation is great. Even if one is married to a perfect partner, one may still want to taste the thrill of a new romance. Extra–marital flings lure spouses to get waylaid. But these may prove to be disastrous for the marriage. Many leave their cosy nests for exotic adventures only to come fluttering home. Within no time they realise that their lover is not and can never be to them what their spouses are - partners for the life and parents to their children. But by then, they had lost the respect of their spouses. The turmoil begins. That lifetime relationship is dented even if the spouse is taken back in the family fold.

Light flings vs Adulterous adventures

A light fling may help to liven up your "slowing" down marital relationship. But these can soon turn into painful and unhappy experiences, for there is a very thin line, which determines the sense of propriety in such relationships, especially for the spouse(s) involved.

Sunaina was visibly happier, more cheerful and exuberant than before. A few minutes of conversation with her revealed that she had found a great company in her colleague Neel. But Sunaina was very clear about her priorities and the extent of her proximity with Neel. With Neel she shared interests like visiting Art galleries and trying new cuisines, which Anant, her husband could never share with her. He had no taste for art or cuisine. There may have been some romantic moments with Neel as they shared the same tastes and enjoyed each other's company. But Sunaina was clear that she was not putting her marriage on the block. "I have never got physical with Neel. Nor has Neel ever insisted to go beyond sharing our common interests," confided Sunaina. Both came to share their interests with each other and respect each others' limits. This brought excitement in Sunaina's otherwise boring marital life.

Sunaina shared, "I knew I was on the edge, but within the boundary, I set for myself; no doubt it was hard to keep and it took a lot of strength to stay this side. But, I did. I knew otherwise it would rip my marriage apart."

Mira Kirshenbaum, an American psychotherapist with 30 years experience in marriage counselling, in her recent book "When Good People Have Affairs", has reportedly stated that the "right kind" of affair can have a positive effect. You could think of it as a necessary medical procedure. If your marriage is in cardiac arrest, an affair can be a defibrillator."

Adulterous involvement however, could be damaging and disastrous, as it hits at the basic foundation of marriage. Attraction for the "forbidden" and "unattainable" is quite natural but it should not be forgotten how devastating this can become. Not because your spouse may find out, but because you may not be able to live with the guilt of it, at some point of time in life.

Sociologist Usha Bambawale[7] says about extra-marital relationships "availability and proximity are the main sources of two human beings getting together. Such people take their marital togetherness as a working relationship. For them, living together and going out together at parties is what constitutes a marriage. That is a peripheral attitude, and one can only see that in couples who live for today as if there is no tomorrow.

... People get into such relationships for short-term pleasure. They ignore the long-term consequences. A day might come when either of the two relationships ends. The marriage goes for a toss. Otherwise, the other relationship is torn apart. Both of them simply cannot co-exist for a long time." .....

Love takes on different forms at different stages of marital life. It may be at its peak one day and may hit the rock bottom, the other day. One cannot have that high intensity affair 24 x 7 x 365. One may not have "passionate sex days" throughout. There are always highs and lows! The troughs in marriage should not be an excuse to indulge outside marriage.

We may have become very liberal outwardly. The stigma attached earlier to adulterous relationships might have been diluted to some extent. But, when such relationship is exposed, it still hurts as much and certainly hits at the foundation of the marital relationship.

Every association to last or to last long, demands mutual faith and trust. So is true of marriage. Infidelity strikes at the very foundation of this association. Infidelity is never forgotten, though it may gradually fade.

I have yet to come across a person, who just shrugged his shoulders at his spouse's extra marital liaison or infidelity saying "it is his/her life!" Although permissiveness is strongly argued to have made great inroads in society, there are hardly any demonstrable instances.

Even in this age of "switching of spouses", It was surprising to hear a business woman and a socialite saying: "I am very careful about relationships now because of my past experiences... People might trust fairytale marriages, but I don't think you can live on fresh air and romance throughout your life! I will settle down only when I meet my soul-mate. I will never compromise and I will never tolerate infidelity. Marriage is for keeps. I'd rather be with someone who I'll spend the rest of my life with, than be with a boyfriend for the moment."

Couples across all strata of society, including those who claim to be "progressive" cannot stand their spouse's extra-marital affairs. Instead, mere suspicion about the spouse's infidelity seems to provoke extreme violence. History is replete with the stories of the jealous spouse killing the paramour.

Nanavati's case

In the year 1959, K.M. Nanavati's case had grabbed the nation's attention. Nanavati, a naval officer killed Prem Ahuja, his wife's paramour. Nanavati was based in Bombay, but being a naval officer, he was frequently away on ship leaving his wife and children at Bombay. In his absence, Nanavati's wife, Sylvia developed proximity with Ahuja, which culminated in illicit intimacy between the two. Nanavati noticed that Sylvia was behaving strangely and was not responsive and affectionate towards him. When questioned, she would evade the issue. One afternoon in April 1959, after lunch, Nanavati questioned Sylvia about her fidelity. She shook her head to indicate that she was unfaithful to him. Nanavati guessed that her paramour was Ahuja. He questioned her on whether Ahuja would marry her and look after the children, but could get no clear answer from her. Enraged, Nanavti decided to settle the matter with Ahuja. He drove Sylvia, their two children and a neighbour's child in his car to a cinema, dropped them there and promised to come and pick them up at 6 p.m., when the show ended. He then drove his car to his ship and drew a revolver from the stores of the ship. From there he went to Ahuja's office, and not finding him there, he drove to Ahuja's flat. He walked in to Ahuja's bedroom and shut the door behind him. Nanavati called Ahuja a filthy swine and asked him whether he would marry Sylvia and look after the children. Ahuja is said to have retorted "Am I to marry every woman I sleep with?" Nanavati was infuriated and shot Ahuja dead.

A farmer reacts the same way

In yet another reported case of 1950's, a farmer saw his wife cohabiting with his bitter enemy; that night he ate no meals; next morning he went to the ryots to get his wages from them, and while going there he saw his wife sharing a meal with her paramour; he killed the paramour then and there. The paramour's conduct was considered by the court to be a grave and sudden provocation to kill him. The court had observed, "With that act, all regard for husband's feelings were abandoned and that they purposed continuing their course of misconduct in his house; this amounted to provocation, grave enough and sudden enough to deprive him of his self control" and reduced the offence from murder to culpable homicide not amounting to murder.

An engineer, no different

Not long ago, Infosys Engineer, allegedly killed his wife, after an argument over her alleged affair with a colleague and therafter committed suicide.

Very recently, a naval officer allegedly killed in a fit of rage, his girlfriend's boss on suspecting him of having an unwarranted liaison with his girlfriend .

Whether it was a farmer in early fifties or a naval officer, Nanavati in 1959 or allegedly an engineer or a naval officer in the twenty first century, (case is still pending decision) things have not changed much. Infidelity evokes the same violent reaction. This is proof enough that howsoever liberal we might have become, infidelity still strikes at the root of the relationship called marriage.

These life situations reinforce that infidelity hits at the root of the marital relationship irrespective of the caste, class or the strata of society, one belongs to.

Before plunging into any relationship outside matrimony, it would be wise to ask oneself if one is ready for the consequences. Whether one is ready to face one's children? Certain attractions may be too strong to resist, but the choice is one's own. It should not happen that one loses the spouse, kids, home and the lover too, who may have his/ her own family, to whom he/ she might be highly attached.

Infidelity proves disastrous

Rameshwar and Kiran, belonged to lower middle class. They were married for about 6 years. Kiran underwent successive miscarriages. They were without a child till the 6th year of their marriage.

Kiran not only suffered immense mental trauma but also had a lot of spare time to brood over her lost pregnancies. Rameshwar was busy with his tailoring shop and hardly had any time to share Kiran's emotional setback. Ali, who was working in Rameshwar's shop as an assistant, used to visit their house sometimes. There was a spark between Ali and Kiran. Kiran found an outlet. She started meeting Ali at his friend's place. They started exchanging letters. Kiran would often leave the house on the pretext of going to the market, oblivious of the fact that she was under observation of her mother-in-law, who got suspicious about her movements. More so, because Kiran's sulks had disappeared. She appeared very lively, when she returned home after "marketing". Once, Kiran left for the market and did not return for 3-4 hours. Rameshwar, by chance visited the house as he needed a piece of cloth. Rameshwar, who till then had not paid much attention to the reports about Kiran leaving the house quite often, was alerted. Rameshwar sent his brother to look for Kiran in the market, which was at a stone's throw distance. Kiran was ultimately traced along with Ali at his friend's house. And, that was it! Although Rameshwar's brother and other family members tried to play down the whole episode but Rameshwar was adamant that Kiran's conduct was intolerable. Rameshwar and Kiran still lived together for about 6-7 months after that incident, but things were never the same, as Rameshwar suspected that Kiran was still continuing with her liaison.

Rameshwar ultimately pronounced his verdict that he was unable to pull on with Kiran anymore. Entreaties of both the families, apology tendered by Kiran, assurances et al, nothing worked.

Rameshwar ultimately filed a petition for dissolution of marriage on the ground of adultery. He was fully equipped with armoury – love letters exchanged between Kiran and Ali, his own mother, brother and a shopkeeper as witnesses.

Even during divorce proceedings, Kiran pleaded that she wanted to save her marriage at all costs. She was ready to give any undertaking, which satisfied Rameshwar. All efforts made by the court, family members and even by the counsellor to save the marriage did not work, as Rameshwar was determined to seek divorce.

Love's labour lost

It was love's labour lost in the case of the Doctor couple Neha Kapoor and Amit Kapoor. They had two sons, aged about 12 years and 8 years.

Neha had her own clinic. Amit was working with a government hospital. Neha developed propinquity with her elder son's tutor. Over a period of time, she even established physical relationship with the tutor. This did not remain a secret for too long. Amit got a wind of it. But the worst happened, when their younger son chanced to witness Neha and the tutor in a compromising position. Amit was startled to hear it from the child's mouth. There was a fierce argument between Neha and Amit. Amit walked out of the house in a rage, as the house they were staying in was inherited by Neha from her parents. Amit also took with him the younger son. Amit started spying on Neha through a private detective agency to gather evidence. Amit even managed to obtain video clips of Neha and the tutor in the act, in the couple's bedroom.

Armed with all this evidence, Amit filed a petition for dissolution of their marriage on the ground of adultery and cruelty. He filed the video recording of his wife and her lover, in support of his case. He even requested the court for allowing him to produce his younger son as a witness, pleading that the child was an eye witness. Perhaps feeling cheated and victimised, Amit lost all concern for other humane aspects.

There were allegations and counter allegations. This litigation not only embarrassed and hurt the spouses and proved disastrous for their marriage, but also for the impressionable children. There was a battle for custody of children. Neha filed a petition that she be given custody of both the children. Amit strongly objected to it contending that Neha was not fit to be a good mother because of her extra-marital sexual adventures. The children were also called by the guardianship court to assess whose guardianship would best serve their welfare.

Amit and Neha agreed to part ways amicably, as a result of counselling and with the intervention of the Delhi High Court. Amit's divorce petition was subsequently converted into a petition for divorce by mutual consent.

Amit and Neha were divorced but their fight to show each other down not only resulted in emotional upheaval for the children but also adversely affected their psyche, their self esteem and confidence.

Children draw pride in their parents' success. Children generally brag about their parents' status. But extra marital involvement of either of the parents and its aftermath, can prove devastating for them. It erodes them of their pride and dignity.

How many lives are at stake, by one act of a wayward spouse? If one feels disgruntled in a relationship, one should talk it over and walk out of the relationship instead of finding succour elsewhere, while continuing with one's matrimony.

Infidelity is hardly tolerated. Exceptions may be there, because of certain circumstances compelling the suffering spouse to continue with the relationship.

Intolerance for infidelity cuts across different cultures in the world; it is not taken kindly to even in the most progressive of societies, if recent newspaper reports were to be believed.

A newspaper[8] recently reported that Malaysian women whose husbands cheated on them are increasingly opting to have affairs of their own called "tit for tat". Most of them do it out of anger at being cheated by their husbands. Suspicious husbands, on the other hand, are calling for more genetic tests on new borns.

In Guangzhou, China, a lush affluent region where adultery is ingrained and wealthy businessmen generally keep their lovers in "concubine villages", infidelity was often tolerated in marriage. However, now girls are opting out of marriage and calling it quits on unfaithful husbands.[9]

A national daily[10] recently reported that to take revenge on her cheating husband, an Australian woman put on e Bay, a photograph of his lover's underpants and an empty condom wrapper found in her bed, after her husband had an affair with another woman. Not only this, she even gave an unflattering description of the knickers. "They are so huge. I thought they may make someone a nice shawl or, even better, something for Halloween perhaps." To embarrass her husband, she even gave a detailed account of the events leading up to the "discovery". Inessa Jackson, a spokeswoman for e Bay said this is obviously very therapeutic for this woman and it must be a great channel for her views on cheating and the sanctity of marriage.

Proximity with boss – may prove disastrous

Encounters with the opposite sex are unavoidable in today's world but the extent of proximity can surely be controlled.

It is wonderful to have a good boss. Nothing beats a friendly and a considerate boss. You are blessed to have a good husband and a good boss too. What more could one ask for, if one has peace and happiness at home and in office too. But sometimes, you may find it hard to stay focused on your family, when you find a great friend in your boss; you may find yourself enjoying his company during official trips, office parties and the time spent together in office. But it is equally true that the boss's goodness, his dropping you home, sending SMS's and sharing lewd jokes, may not be taken too kindly by your husband.

Tanya, a beautiful girl, was a computer engineer. She had an arranged marriage with Pradeep, and they had been married for about five years. Tanya belonged to Delhi and was working with a software company in Delhi. Pradeep was from Chandigarh and was a senior executive with a multinational company. After marriage, they stayed together for sometime at Chandigarh with Pradeep's parents. Thereafter, Pradeep was transferred to Mumbai. Tanya shuttled between Mumbai & Chandigarh. She then decided to re-join her job at Delhi. Tanya had also conceived by that time. Tanya and Pradeep remained in touch over phone and sometimes Pradeep would stop over at Delhi on his official trips. This arrangement continued till Tanya delivered a baby boy. Pradeep wanted her to shift to Chandigarh to his parent's place. Tanya felt more comfortable at her parent's place. This led to some misgivings in the mind of her in-laws. However, they reluctantly agreed with the arrangement.

Tanya resumed her job after a brief sabbatical of two months. Pradeep would request Tanya to visit his parents at Chandigarh. Tanya would always have some reason for not visiting Chandigarh, like– the baby was small, she could not take leave and so on. The separation and unhappiness over Tanya's reluctance to move out of Delhi led to a strain between Tanya and Pradeep. Pradeep, at that juncture was successful in getting a transfer to Ludhiana. Tanya joined him at Ludhiana for some time. She however continued with her job at Delhi. She would travel to Ludhiana on weekends, leaving the child with her parents at Delhi, as there was no one to take care of the child at Ludhiana.

One day, at about midnight, the SMS beep of Tanya's cell phone woke Pradeep. Pradeep could not control his curiosity to check the sender at that unearthly hour. Pradeep was upset after reading the SMS. It was a lewd joke sent by Tanya's boss at that late hour. Pradeep did not say anything about it but could not be at peace after that incident. Thereafter, Tanya had to visit Singapore for a week in connection with a sales project. Her boss also accompanied Tanya on that official trip. Pradeep did not say anything, as he was himself bogged down with official assignments. A few days after the trip, Pradeep again happened to peek into SMS's received by Tanya from her boss. One of them shocked Pradeep. It read "..... I can't forget that evening stroll at Singapore Mall.... that moonlit night.... I look forward to many such trips together..."

Pradeep was deeply hurt. He kept awake one night and downloaded and printed all the SMSs sent by Tanya's boss to her. He then confronted Tanya with that. She was taken aback. "...there is nothing between me and my boss......, you need not imagine anything beyond these SMSs. He just shares these funny jokes and nothing more...", explained Tanya.

This explanation could not convince Pradeep. He met Tanya's father and showed him all those SMSs. Tanya's father tactfully handled the situation and assured Pradeep that he will take up the matter with Tanya. Ultimately, Tanya's father convinced her to seek transfer to some other office. She attempted to get a change, but was unsuccessful, as the marketing job was available only at Delhi. Pradeep asked Tanya to resign and told her that he would get her an equally good job at Ludhiana or in a nearby town. But Tanya refused. The issue snowballed. Tanya continued to stay at Delhi, Pradeep at Ludhiana. Suspicion and strain were aggravated by physical distance between the two.

Both the families made efforts to bring them together, but without any positive result. Ultimately, Pradeep filed a petition for dissolution of marriage on the ground of cruelty. He reproduced SMSs sent by Tanya's boss and pleaded cruelty and infidelity.

During the divorce proceedings, repeated efforts were made for removing misgivings between Tanya and Pradeep. Pradeep's point was that Tanya still continued to share undue familiarity with her boss and that is why she refused to leave her job. Tanya's plea was that she would be totally insecure and would be robbed of her financial security, if she left her job and if Pradeep also decided to leave her subsequently. None of them was ready to relent. Ultimately with the help of parents from both sides, a positive role played by both the lawyers and as a result of counselling by the court, a middle path was worked out. Tanya took three months leave from her job and joined Pradeep in Ludhiana. Both were to look for some equally remunerative job for Tanya in Ludhiana. The child's schooling in Delhi continued.

Although, Pradeep succumbed to friends' and family's pressure to join Tanya, but he was deeply hurt and still felt that Tanya had cheated on him. Both joined each other with a promise to forget the past, to look forward in life and to take a break and go for a long vacation together. It is not known what happened thereafter. With time and genuine efforts, I hope that they regained their old relationship.

It may be natural to develop proximity with peers and bosses, with whom one may be spending long hours and may share a great equation. Physical absence of spouse at the same time might give an added opportunity to go a little further, but it is important to ask whether you would tolerate the same thing if your spouse were in your place.

In the present era of long working hours, the reasons for affinity with peer group including opposite sex, are not hard to find. Soma Shekhar, a thirty year old software engineer from a conservative Tamil Brahmin family, had an arranged marriage two years ago. He was spending more than 11 hours of his waking time at work. He was too busy moving up the corporate ladder and hardly had any time to spend with his wife, Annarathi. Moreover he felt, it was only his colleagues who could understand the pulls and pressures of his life. All his relationships revolved around his office. Soma Shekhar admitted that "It's work, where we socialise, make friends, look for support in weaker moments and even for love. After long working hours, when I return home, I am hardly left with any energy. Whatever time I get, is spent on catching up with sleep..."

Office has become all-consuming. Colleagues are gradually taking the place of friends, families and sometimes even the wife or husband.

Companionship at work place

"If it wasn't for an official tour, I may not have realised my tilt towards Dhruv. Dhruv and I found that we share a great equation," said Neeraja. The long hours at work may explain why working spouses are looking to colleagues for companionship. In case of those coming from orthodox families, such affairs at work are liberating and meet their search for freedom and self worth.

Anita, a TV journalist, has to stay out on night shifts. Such continuous night shifts have ensured that she spends more time with her colleagues than her husband. She frankly admitted, "There is so much temptation to stray because of long hours and attractive and understanding colleagues. You tend to be close to your colleagues, in weaker moments.... But I know where to call it quits..."

The fact that one's innocuous proximity may embarrass and hurt one's spouse, should not be lost sight of. It is great to share warm relationship with like-minded people at work, but one should be clear, as to how far one wants to go. Sensitivity of the spouse should not be forgotten, lest one's heavenly cocoon is shattered. One may not want to lose an equally warm relationship with one's spouse.

Ignorance: Not bliss

It is good to have mutual trust and not to unnecessarily suspect the spouse's camaraderie. But there have been instances where ignorance, deliberate or otherwise has landed people in trouble.

Namita was shocked to receive a notice of divorce case filed by her husband Kamal, with whom she had been living till three days back, when he left for some "official assignment". They had even been sharing a normal sexual relationship.

Namita was at her wit's end, when she came to know that Kamal had developed a relationship with her close friend Rakshita. Namita then recalled, "I did not have any inkling of what was coming my way..... Now I remember, I had lightly objected to Kamal's flirtatious remarks towards Rakshita, when she had come over for dinner at our house..... Kamal had given me a peck on my cheek and had hugged me and that was it! I could not suspect what was going on......"

Inroads by own sister

The story of Ammu was still more disturbing. Ammu delivered a baby girl by c-section, after a year of her marriage. Her unmarried younger sister, Reena came to help her through this tough time. Ammu was more than involved with the baby. Reena took charge of Ammu's kitchen, packing Shashank's tiffin etc. Ammu mistook Reena and Shashank's growing proximity for camaraderie. Ammu recounted, "...After about a month Reena left and everything returned to normal. I was in command of the house. Both of us were quite happy with our marriage and grown family till the day, when I chanced to pick up the receiver from the parallel telephone line. The ground slipped from under my feet, when I heard Shashank and Reena's conversation. I was shell shocked even to react and to confront Shashank.

After Shashank left for office, I went straight to my Mom's house and shared that information with her in private. Initially, my Mom refused to believe and tried hard to convince me that there must have been some misunderstanding or it might simply be figment of my imagination. Ultimately, Mom had to agree with me, when Reena did not deny her affection for Shashank.

The worst came, when my own mother despite her best efforts could not dissuade Reena. Reena conveyed that she was ready to share my household and Shashank with me, if I permitted her to do so. There was no question of my agreeing to that. I told Shashank in clear terms, it is either me or her. Shashank decided to walk out of our marriage, magnanimously offering to provide support to me and our daughter.

I could not take it. I went into depression, lost 15 kg of weight and the desire to live. It took me a long time to recover and collect the pieces of my life and start again...."

Meenakshi also meets the same fate.

Something similar happened in the case of Meenakshi and Mihir. Meenakshi and Mihir were both in government jobs. They had two teenage daughters. Meenakshi confided, "Mihir developed unwarranted proximity with my sister. Initially he denied any such liasion but he left us and started living with my sister in a rented accommodation, when nagging increased. I spoke with my mother, but she also expressed her helplessness.

... My daughters remained in touch with Mihir over phone. Initially, Mihir would even sometimes visit my daughters at home... But steadily his visits home stopped; he would ask my daughters to meet him at some restaurant. Things continued this way. One day through a common acquaintance, I came to know that a son has been born to him, out of his relationship with my sister.

.....I was totally shattered by the news of my sister bearing a child out of her relationship with my husband. But thinking of my daughters' future, I again collected myself and requested my mother to intervene. My mother, instead of sympathasising with me, started preaching and sermonising me and asked me to adjust. She ordained me not to create fuss and not to make an issue of out of it, or else my sister and her child's life would be ruined. The earth under my feet slipped. I felt nauseated at my mother's suggestion......

My daughters are growing up. They feel embarrassed talking about their father but nevertheless they miss him a lot, being very attached to him. Of late, Mihir's phone calls to my daughters have reduced; same has started affecting my daughters not only emotionally but also in their studies.

......Despite Mihir's conduct, I spoke with him for my daughters' sake. I pleaded with him to return home. I even told him that he may not keep any relation with me and may live in a separate room. I even suggested to him that he may bring his son along, if he wanted; I will raise that child also. Mihir made it clear that he will not return home, come what may. Mihir remained unmoved.

All my pleas that my daughters' future shall be ruined... who will marry daughters of such a father?, simply fell on deaf ears. He kept on insisting that our daughters were free to meet him, whenever and wherever they wanted."

Meenakshi had filed a petition for restitution of conjugal rights. Mihir did not budge from his stand even during the counselling session. He offered to help the daughters with their studies and was ready to contribute for their wedding but nothing beyond that.

Many such cases revealed that generally spouses instinctively sense when the other is straying but still buy excuses probably because they are unsure of themselves, whether they would be able to take this to logical conclusion; whether they can choose to break, if the other admits and refuses to discontinue. Those not confident of themselves choose to look the other way; prefer to turn a blind eye to the spouse's dalliance. Because by accepting the fact, they will have to face the situation.

Looking the other way

Nayanika was better looking than Kishore. She was vivacious, outgoing and full of life whereas, Kishore was more of a recluse. He preferred the quiet of the house and loved reading classics. Nayanika enjoyed partying and dancing. But their distinct tastes were never a problem. They still made a good match, as Kishore was a caring husband and loving father and did not mind Nayanika enjoying her parties alone. Both progressed well in their careers.

Nayanika gelled well with Raman, one of her colleagues, who also shared her interests. Nayanika strayed. Kishore sensed that something was amiss. He knew about Nayanika's dalliance but surprisingly preferred to look the other way; perhaps Kishore loved Nayanika so much that he was unprepared to deal with emotional turmoil consequent to their break up. His life revolved around Nayanika and their daughter Neha. He did not want to disturb the fabric of his life by having to deal with Nayanika's waywardness. Kishore did not take Nayanika's distraction as his rejection. He realised that he was not able to match her energy and was unable to accompany her to all the outings and parties, she loved and enjoyed.

Some are lucky few to have sailed through such an affair, after confronting the spouse. Deliberately looking the other way may prove blissful sometimes! Yet, not many have the courage to pull on with patience and deliberation for so many years before confrontation.

No one can say, whether confronting the spouse instantly would help or ignoring it would be better. Giving oneself time and mustering courage to deal with it, appears to be a better option. It may allow the spouse to realise that you value your marriage and are prepared to work on it. But, it all depends upon one's own take on marriage.

Trespassers beware

Indifference or too much of possessiveness can hamper the relationship and can even lead to break-ups. Relationships are based on love, trust and respect for each other. A possessive streak can open the relationship to a whole new world of anger, outrage and insane behaviour.

If you rub shoulders with the rich and famous, and your profession entails socialising at glamorous locales, it constantly threatens your partner.

If your good looks are not complemented by the looks of your partner and you become the centre of attraction wherever you go, your relationship may be the hub of grave insecurities. An average looking partner may constantly cringe under the fear of losing his better half to a more attractive person. Such a partner can make life rather difficult for the other person in the relationship.

Spouse's insecurity can be pain

Neeta, a beautiful outgoing girl from North-east, was living in the University Hostel. Akshat was part of Neeta's circle of friends, who were preparing for a competitive examination. Neeta was just friends with Akshat like other members of her gang. But somewhere down the line Akshat got interested in Neeta beyond their friendship. Akshat sent feelers to Neeta. Neeta did not take much note of it. Akshat started getting desperate, with the passage of time. He made every effort to persuade Neeta to marry him. He then sought the help of Madhav, the most sensible member of the group. Neeta had not really thought about marriage till then and tried to put that across to Akshat. But Akshat was steadfast. Akshat's persistent efforts through common friends ultimately made Neeta rethink. Neeta ultimately thought that she had to get married one day and Akshat was not a bad person. She gave her consent at last. Both got married about a year later.

Things were pretty normal between Neeta and Akshat for about 8-10 months of their marriage. Neeta was the same bubbly, tweety and outgoing person. She was the same old Neeta for her group. Akshat was little distraught about Neeta meeting Raman, Madhav and other members of their old gang in the same warm manner, as she always used to. He subtly conveyed this to Neeta. Neeta just laughed it off initially, assuring Akshat not to feel threatened. But that apparent childish jealousy took on monstrous proportions over next one year of their marriage.

Neeta had picked up a job and generally used to be back home before Akshat. Neeta missed her chartered bus once and got delayed by about an hour. Akshat was restless. Akshat started off with his interrogation the moment Neeta entered the house. Neeta was shocked at Akshat's reaction, as she was expecting sympathy and consolation from Akshat for the trouble she had to undergo in travelling by public transport. She was numbed by Akshat's remark "Why only you missed the chartered bus?"

"What do you mean to say?" screamed Neeta.

Neeta and Akshat did not share a word with each other for a few days. Ultimately, Neeta thought there was no point taking it too far, as that was spoiling the atmosphere at home. "I am not running away with anyone." She told Akshat in a lighter vein, sensing his insecurity. Things became normal after sometime.

But this episode was the reflection of things coming Neeta's way.

At a batch party, Neeta was as excited as she could be, just reliving the past. She was as bindas and as outgoing as she used to be, shaking hands and hugging old friends. Akshat withdrew into his shell and was formal in his interaction with everyone. Akshat remained withdrawn for few days. Neeta could not simply fathom the reason.

A few days later, Akshat came to pick up Neeta at her office; on their way back, they stopped at a provision store. While Neeta went to pick up some grocery, Akshat continued sitting in the car. All of a sudden, Neeta found Akshat honking incessantly. She hurriedly returned, picking up the purchased stuff. "What happened?" No sooner had Neeta asked Akshat, he blasted like a suppressed volcano "What was taking you so long? For a simple purchase of few grocery items you take ages. What was going on!! Were you purchasing grocery or (were you) sharing jokes?"

Neeta was nonplussed. She could hardly make any sense out of Akshat's outburst. "I was kind of brain dead for few moments. I fought with Akshat on reaching home. But he was just the same. He told me that he is not a fool and understands everything. "What everything?" I had screamed. We did not share the bedroom for about a week. But how long could we continue like this. I am what I am. The gloomy atmosphere gets on my nerves. I was and am a simple fun loving, honest person. There were moments, when I thought of breaking loose. But friends persuaded me not to act in haste. On other occasions, the thought of my daughter shook the mother inside me and dissuaded me from depriving my daughter of fatherly love. Akshat otherwise, is a good person and doting father.

There were many more such incidents. So many times, I decided that I cannot put up pretences. I can't stop talking to my old friends or laughing with them. At one point of time, I even felt like ending my life. I couldn't do that even.

With time, I realised that he is too possessive of me; his jealousy and imaginary proximity between me and my male friends stems from nothing but his own insecurity of losing me. I have come to terms with it and have found my own way to handle it. I watch my behaviour, when I am with my male friends. You can call it the price, I am paying for peace at home.

This is the way, we are "happily" married for about the last 25 years" shared Neeta.

It is difficult to change one's nature overnight. But being conscious that too much possessiveness does not pay in any sphere in life, helps.

Don't bring official attitude home

The other trait which might ruin ones' marriage is expecting of your spouse, obedience of the kind which you receive at your workplace.

During counselling in the petition for restitution of conjugal rights filed by Ajit, Sayli disclosed that she was undergoing treatment for depression. She confided, "Being a senior manager in a leading ad agency, Ajit's attitude towards perfectionism was something he simply brought home from work. He called me inefficient and incapable of doing anything right (in his opinion); that is what hurt me the most and eroded me of my self-confidence."

"... I was a gold medalist and an all rounder and all time favourite of one and all in my school. Ajit made me feel worthless, every moment he was with me. I started doubting my own capabilities. Since, I believed that the situation and circumstances were impossible, I walked out. But that did not end my misery; I slipped into depression. With constant support and sympathy of my parents and my friends, I am on the path of recovery. The very thought of Ajit's company, sends chills down my spine and makes me nervous. I can't even think of talking to him what to talk of joining him at this stage."

Ajit's case for restitution of conjugal rights was still pending, as Sayali had refused to join him.

A husband needs to treat his wife as an individual first and then as a partner; the fact that everyone has a distinct personality needs to be appreciated. The spouse's individuality needs to be respected; but traditionally, it is the men who decide for the family; women's assertiveness is not appreciated.

Rachna shared, "Although, I enjoyed staying at home and spending time with my children, my husband Ritwik insisted that I should take up a job, after our kids were 4 and 6 years of age. Compelled by Ritwik and his parents, I took up a job half-heartedly. I felt miserable at work, missing my children all through the day. At home, Ritwik wasn't happy with me, as I could not do well at my job. Ultimately, I had to quit my job which added fuel to the fire...... I lost confidence in myself. I was not able to take any decision without Ritwik's reaffirmation. I needed reassurance at every step. I felt absolutely worthless. This lowered me in my own eyes. Depression set in over a period of time, without my realising it.

... But for my childhood friend, I would have become a nervous wreck. With God's grace, timely treatment and counselling helped me."

Marriage does not work unless both the wheels are on an even keel. Both are crucial for a smooth journey. But, housewives are generally taken for granted by their spouses and even by their children. A woman's self confidence might plummet because of a hyper critical husband. She may not realise that the problem is not with her, but with her husband.

Honesty: The bedrock

Like respect for each other, honesty in the relationship sustains marital bond. Honesty is the foundation of any long lasting relationship. But, does honesty mean that one must go ahead and bare one's chest indiscriminately?

Sharing experience of a premarital fling with one's life partner to unburden one's conscience may not be a bad idea; but before one does that one should see the level of maturity of the spouse. It should not happen that the disclosure about one's harmless, immature infatuation with a boy or the girl next door kills one's marriage. There is no point giving too much importance to that liaison. Not disclosing does not mean being dishonest towards the partner. What matters is honesty in the present relationship.

One must understand the gravity of the "truth" being disclosed, keeping in mind the repercussions that might follow. One should be careful enough to discern "what" and "how- much" should be disclosed. There is no point telling one's spouse something, which one knows could cause a rift in one's relationship. Revealing an innocuous and frivolous detail of your life is simply foolish. In the long run, this may do more harm than good to the marital relationship.

Not sharing a plain stupid crush is not being hypocrite.

So many times, you must have been thoroughly put off at the arrival of your in-laws, who chose to land at your place right before your children's examinations. But you might have feigned such a warm welcome, as if you were just dying to meet them. That is not being dishonest but only acting wise, so is keeping your premarital life to yourself. Such off-track flings are best kept with you, as talking about them may not only embarrass your spouse but may also hurt your marriage.

Unless, there is a decent level of understanding between the two, such revelations are bound to offend one's spouse. Some men are just not brought up that way. They carry such disclosures like extra baggage, which may be dropped on you when you are at a 'low' in your relationship. It would be most hurting then.

Innocuous disclosure – sowed seeds of suspicion

Renu, an old college friend was going steady with Deepak, a class mate for about a year. By their final year of M.A., both grew out of their relationship and realised that they had different ways to go. After M.A., while Renu was preparing for M. Phil, she came in contact with Arun. They were simply friends. But Arun got serious and sent a message through a common friend, if Renu would consider a serious relationship. Renu was reluctant. But, Arun got a little too serious and she was kind of persuaded to say 'yes'. They had a courtship of about 2-3 years. Renu was always easy going – happy-go-lucky. After marriage, Arun started subtly expressing his dislike for her free mingling with other male friends.

Once in a great mood, Renu just talked to Arun about her fling with Deepak. That was it! Thereafter, Arun got so suspicious about her that every friendly interaction of hers with the opposite sex, was seen with tinted eyes. This sometimes led to sulks and sometimes to subtle taunts. Sometimes, Renu would be told in clear terms, "Why those guys get friendly only with you?" Renu would feel offended by such remarks. This would often lead to heated arguments between them.

Renu's simple sharing of her college time fling sowed seeds of suspicion in her marital relationship. She told, "I did not want to hide anything and why should I? I never did anything wrong in my life. Moreover I never proposed to Arun. He only was after my life to marry him. He can't choose my friends."

What was the need for Renu to share with Arun, something which lost its meaning much before she tied the knot with Arun? Not revealing such one off affair, is not being dishonest. Such "confession", if it can be termed so, can cause death blow to the relationship. Men being extremely possessive by nature, cannot accept that their spouse shared equally warm relationship with someone else, even at some point of time in the past; and irrespective of the fact that it was a plain infatuation or madness. Such confessions do not help either of the spouses.

When you are stepping into a new life long relationship, all previous associations are best buried and their pug marks left covered. Else, the past can turn out to be an unwelcome intrusion into your current relationship. Honesty in existing relationship is what matters the most. If that is there, nothing can beat it.

***

♥ Much preparation is made for wedding rituals and fanfare associated with it; but there is hardly any preparation for embracing the new role and set up.

- ♥ Marriage needs constant work and investment of time & emotion to keep the romance alive.
- ♥ Sense the signals of alienation and take charge, lest it is too late.
- ♥ Communication, maintaining physical touch and small kind gestures towards spouse, keep freshness and romance alive.
- ♥ Respect the views and feelings of spouse, howsoever different and beyond comprehension, they may be.
- ♥ Develop your hobbies and pursue your own interests alongside.
- ♥ Adulterous alliances in the family or beyond, may be exhilarating for a while, but may kill your marriage, as infidelity is not tolerated.
- ♥ Honesty in the relationship is a sine qua non for its survival and beauty.

4

WHAT AILS MARRIAGE: THE INDIAN PECULIARITIES

Everything will be Alright after Marriage

Many marriages break within no time and for reasons which I feel, are peculiar to 'Indian' society. There is a general belief in our country that everything will be all right after marriage. If the boy is a vagabond, does not earn, does not care for his responsibilities, pat would come the advise, "Get him married, he will stop loitering and will become responsible". The boy is married off ignoring the writing on the wall.

Not disclosing previous ailment and significant medical history of the boy or the girl is also a common tendency amongst the Indians. Despite knowing fully-well that one may have to pay a heavy price for this indiscreetness, every effort is made to hide rather than reveal the deformity or ailment which the boy or the girl suffers from. Such an attitude is anathema to marriage and building up of the bond.

Concealment of doping habit

Anirudh's parents, despite being well aware that Anirudh has taken to drugs and has stopped going to work regularly, decided to marry him. Once married, Anirudh's wife will wean him off drugs; family responsibilities will compel Anirudh to take his work seriously, thought Anirudh's parents. Anirudh was good looking, and was a part of flourishing family business which was actually managed by his father and elder brother. Finding a suitable match for him was not a problem. The unwary parents of Kavya, happily agreed for the alliance. Their inquiries from a common acquaintance did not reveal, what they should have known about Anirudh before getting into the alliance.

The marriage was solemnised. Everything was fine for about a month. Kavya could not sense Anirudh's doping habit, but when Anirudh started returning late at night in a "high" condition, she did smell that something was amiss. She still could not imagine that Anirudh was addicted to drugs. Anirudh wouldn't get up till noon; his trips to the shop were getting few and far between.

After about two to three months of her marriage, Kavya to her horror, discovered that her gold chain was missing. Kavya kept searching for it, without disclosing it to anyone thinking that she might have misplaced it somewhere. She ultimately informed her mother-in-law, when she could not locate her chain despite utmost efforts. Her mother-in-law did not react much to this news, contrary to what was expected by Kavya. Kavya was impressed by her mother-in-law's cool and composed attitude. But that was not to be for too long!

Kavya was shell shocked the next day, when she overheard her ma-in-law scolding Anirudh, "You shameless fellow, you had promised to give up. You have not spared your wife even. It can't go on like this...." Then, it was revealed to Kavya that Anirudh was addicted to drugs and had sold her gold chain, when he did not get money from elsewhere for the dope.

"I was totally shattered but it was not easy for me to walk out of marriage, as I was already in the family way; there was no scope for termination of pregnancy even; I was very much afraid to go it alone. I somehow came to terms with this revelation and started making efforts to wean Anirudh off drugs. Anirudh also promised to get out of it. But one day, I found him putting iodex on the bread and eating.... promises were made and broken..... he would leave it and get into it again; I came across an NGO, which ran a de-addiction camp. It was a residential camp of 2-3 weeks duration. I managed to persuade Anirudh to give it a shot. But all my efforts were brought to naught, when my mother-in-law screamed at me and told that Anirudh will not attend that camp. She said that she had heard a lot about ill treatment meted out to patients at such camps...."

"Anirudh thus, did not attend that camp.... things went on like that.... That was not the end. After I gave birth to a baby girl and our expenses increased, I was subjected to taunts, "Your husband is good for nothing... he is worthless. You are burden on the family, et al." To compensate for Anirudh's shortcomings, I used to work from dawn to dusk, making every possible effort not to give any opportunity to anyone to complain. Yet, with time, taunts took the shape of warnings, which then converted into ultimatums to make our own arrangement because Anirudh had stopped working altogether."

I was at crossroads.... did not know what to do. My parents were not well off and my two sisters were yet to be married ... I did not want to be a burden on them.... shamelessly ... crushing my dignity, I continued in my matrimonial home for my daughter's sake. But how long could have I continued like that? "

Irresponsible and deceitful behaviour of Anirudh's parents ruined a life which could have been beautiful. Driven to the wall, Kavya filed a petition for dissolution of her marriage on the grounds of cruelty and concealment of material fact by Anirudh and his parents. Counselling did not work, as Kavya was firm that she had already made the best possible efforts to save her marriage and could not take it anymore. She refused to join the company of Anirudh; her divorce petition was still pending as Anirudh did not agree for divorce by mutual consent; he insisted that he should be given one more chance to mend himself but Kavya was in no mood to relent.

In an arranged marriage, what we generally look for is appearance, education, job, remuneration, etc. of the prospective spouse and then we make inquiries about the family background. Health profile of the life partner is hardly ever asked for. Scriptures provide that persons (both groom and bride) suffering from contagious and incurable diseases like leprosy, insanity etc. or who are addicted to vices like gambling deserve rejection.

Hide and seek what ?

In Rashi's case, hiding a material fact and something so evident, knowing fully-well that it cannot remain a secret for too long, was what proved ruinous. Rashi, a beautiful 19 years old girl was married off by her parents to son of her father's colleague, Rajneesh. Rashi and Rajneesh had hardly met each other before marriage. They only had a formal interaction at some family get-together.

After marriage, Rashi kept avoiding physical proximity with Rajneesh. Rajneesh also did not rush in for the act, thinking that Rashi perhaps needed sometime. However, even after about two weeks of marriage, Rashi still did not take the initiative nor did she allow Rajneesh to indulge. Rajneesh was puzzled. He could not understand Rashi's cold attitude. Somehow, he managed to persuade Rashi to allow physical intimacy. To his horror, Rajneesh found that Rashi did not have the normal vaginal opening. His world came crashing down. Rajneesh did not know what to do!

Rajneesh's frustration was too obvious, to remain a secret from his family members for too long. But Rajneesh did not know how to share something so intimate with his family members. Ultimately, Rajneesh shared the 'fact' with his elder brother, who could not believe it. That was it. There was a furore in the house. The matter was then discussed with Rashi's parents, who insisted that she was normal.

Rajneesh made up his mind that he could not lead a normal married life with Rashi. He left Rashi at her parent's place within a month of their marriage. Rashi's parents consulted a specialist doctor at the All India Institute of Medical Sciences, Delhi (AIIMS). After Rashi's medical examination, the doctor assured that Rashi could lead a perfect married life, after corrective surgery. The doctor informed them that Rashi has absolutely normal and healthy reproductive organs and with the help of a corrective surgery, a vaginal opening could be formed. Rashi could subsequently go in for cosmetic surgery for formation of the physical organ.

Rashi's father approached Rajneesh's family with all those reports but Rajneesh and his parents were not ready to accept any further problems. They felt cheated. Rajneesh filed a petition for divorce and did not relent during counselling. He did not agree to give Rashi a chance to undergo medical treatment.

The blame squarely lies with Rashi's parents for hiding such a crucial fact. They not only ruined Rajneesh's life but also subjected their own daughter to humiliation and indignity.

This was an extreme case of concealment. Non disclosure of some minor but significant fact about the spouse can also lead to a break up.

Material facts, small or big are best revealed

Ruchika, a software engineer was settled in US. Raman, also an engineer was employed with a blue chip company in Mumbai. The match between the two was made through a common friend.

After marriage, Raman shifted to US. Raman filed a petition for divorce at Delhi on the ground that Ruchika and her parents concealed from him and his family members a material fact about Ruchika's mental health.

During counselling, Raman said, "While searching for my handkerchief, I dug into Ruchika's cupboard. On finding some medicine strips in her cupboard, I asked Ruchika about it; instead of responding to my query, Ruchika changed the topic. But I could not kill my curiosity. When Ruchika was away at her parent's place one evening, I looked for those medicines to find out the ailment they were meant for; while hunting for those strips, I came across the doctor's prescription, which revealed that Ruchika was undergoing treatment for some mental ailment for about last 2 years.

... I confronted Ruchika on her return; instead of sharing her health problem with me, she started shouting and screaming at me, "How dare you touch my personal stuff... you lack basic manners..." and threw a paper-weight at me in a fit of rage. I also lost my temper and called her lunatic..."

"I cannot trust her or her parents anymore. How can I spend rest of my life with someone, whom I don't trust...?" Raman quipped.

Ruchika, on the other hand shared, "I had suffered mild depression on account of some problem at my work place. I was under medication for the same, when I got married. It was no big deal and there was nothing worth sharing. The doctor had advised me to continue with the treatment for about a year. Raman unnecessarily got hyper about the whole issue."

Conversation with both the spouses and their family members revealed that there were other issues also between them like parity of status, different life styles, Ruchika's eyesight etc. These were not big issues but Raman got an easy way out through the concealment issue.

Raman was firm about his decision to break-up.

There is no harm in sharing information about one's ailment, big or small, which would require treatment to be continued after marriage. It is better to discuss these issues before getting into an alliance, instead of facing uncompromising attitudes later on, because the break-up on that account subsequent to marriage would be more painful, than before it.

Kavya and Rashi's stories are one end of the spectrum; the other end is, the exaggerated sensitivity of people towards the smallest of ailments of a newly-wed, more so, if the girl is suffering from it.

Hypersensitivity of spouse

Karuna's case was the other extreme. It reflects an absolutely insensitive attitude, a spouse may have towards the other, even though the other spouse might have contacted the infection post-marriage.

Karuna, a school-teacher got married to Ravi, engaged in the business of lubricants. After about 4-5 months of their marriage, Karuna started running mild fever. Recurrent attacks of mild fever, caused concern. Ravi's family doctor advised Karuna to undertake thorough medical examination. Karuna's medical examination revealed presence of HSV Virus. The doctor then advised that Ravi should also go in for tests for the same. But Ravi refused to undergo any medical test.

Karuna's medical report of HSV+ became the harbinger of trouble in her married life. Ravi started questioning her, whether she had this infection even prior to marriage. Karuna was pained by Ravi's disbelief and refusal to accept that she did not have any such infection prior to marriage. Ravi even started avoiding Karuna and physical proximity vanished from their relationship. That was not the end. One day, in a hurry, Karuna burnt a toast. Karuna's mother-in-law scolded "..... We have been cheated. We don't know with who all you had been going around. My son has been trapped. You better not get into my kitchen again...."

Karuna was in tears and looked towards Ravi for support. But she was crestfallen, when Ravi also sided with his mother. Karuna told, "Such taunts increased day by day. One day Ravi, went to the extent of charging that I must have had pre-marital sex with someone to be afflicted with HSV Virus. I could not take insults and indignities, any further. I came back to my parents' house. But I always tried to be in touch with Ravi. My parents also spoke with Ravi and his parents, to clarify. I pleaded with Ravi, to visit a specialist Doctor, to clear all his doubts but he refused point blank.... I then visited AIIMS for a detailed examination. After considering my reports, the doctor told me that I had contacted the infection only recently. The doctor also told that the possibility of getting this infection from Ravi could not be ruled out. Rather, there were very strong chances of the same. The doctor asked me to visit along with Ravi and advised that Ravi should also undergo medical tests for his own safety and that of both of us. I appraised Ravi about that. But Ravi did not relent..."

Ravi filed a petition for dissolution of marriage on the ground of cruelty, pleading concealment by Karuna, of her precarious medical condition. He even pleaded that Karuna must have had premarital sexual relations with someone. Karuna on the other hand pleaded that she had contacted that infection from Ravi. She even mentioned that her recent tests had revealed that she was no more HSV+.

Efforts made for counselling during the divorce proceedings failed. Ravi was not ready to understand that Karuna might have got this infection from him or in any manner other than sexual intercourse. He did not even agree to see a doctor. Ravi's attitude led not only to breaking of marriage but a social stigma on Karuna. Karuna was deeply hurt by Ravi's wild and baseless allegations and also by the taunts and sneers she was subjected to, by his relatives and others.

Assumptions made on the basis of a medical report reflected the immature, chauvinistic and biased attitude of the spouse, which led to break-up.

Somewhat similar was the case of Nalini and Ganesh.

Nalini meets the same fate.

Nalini and Ganesh made a picture perfect match, till I saw Nalini chewing her lips and smiling without reason.

Ganesh had filed a petition for divorce on the ground of "insanity", which was strongly contested by Nalini. During reconciliation proceedings, Ganesh clarified, "It is not possible for me to live with Nalini anymore. I have been cheated into this relationship. Nalini's parents did not disclose before marriage that she underwent treatment for insanity. She gets up in the middle of the night and starts howling.... at times she would keep calling me in the office while I would be in the midst of a meeting and would impress upon me to come home immediately... once she bolted herself in the bathroom and threatened to jump down... How can I live in peace in her company? I don't want myself to turn lunatic."

Nalini's father insisted that with regular treatment Nalini would be absolutely normal. He told, "...We did not hide anything. Nalini had slipped into mild depression due to academic burden, when she was in 12th standard. But with treatment, she recovered fully.... Rather, she scored 92% marks and topped in 3 subjects. She is a gold medalist in BA (History). She had a brilliant academic record. She used to excel even in extracurricular activities.... Where was the occasion to disclose a one off incident of depression, she suffered 5 years prior to her marriage.

She was absolutely normal at the time of marriage. But subtle demands of dowry, incessant taunts about quality of dowry items and constantly being ridiculed for lack of culinary skills, took its toll on Nalini. Ganesh's indifference in all these matters added fuel to the fire. This was not the end. By giving birth to a girl child

Nalini evoked further wrath of her mother-in-law... Nalini had lost her mother two years before her marriage; she did not share all these things with me. I could also not sense the gravity of mental torture, Nalini was being subjected to... As a result of all this, Nalini slipped into depression. The indifferent attitude of Ganesh caused further harm to her fragile health condition...

One fine morning, they dumped Nalini at my house announcing that they can't take care of my "mad" daughter any more. Nalini received another shock, when Ganesh snatched the daughter from her saying that a mad mother can't take care of their daughter. Nalini could not bear the pain of separation from her daughter and had subsequently slipped into severe depression.

By God's grace, she has now recovered fully. But, she can't take the emotional trauma of separation from her child and husband any more. The doctor has advised that she should get the company of both, or else she might slip into the same state of health."

Ganesh was adamant that he could not live with Nalini, as he had been cheated into this alliance. Doctor's testimony that anyone undergoing emotional turbulence can slip into depression and that Nalini was able to lead an absolutely normal life with some follow up treatment, could not persuade Ganesh to join Nalini.

It is commonplace, even among educated people to put blame on girl, if she is not able to conceive till a few years after marriage. The husband would generally not undergo medical tests, even though advised by the doctor. There have been cases where husbands' low sperm count or any other health condition was responsible for not be-getting a child but wives were blamed for the same and were branded as "bānjh" (infertile). The same attitude continues with other ailments and problems. All the blame is placed on the girl, with the husband refusing medical checkups or taking responsibility for causing the trouble.

Small ailment: Big issue

There is a tendency amongst in-laws to carry out microscopic examination of daughter-in-law's ailments, small or big, insignificant or significant and to make an issue out of it.

Rhea, a 22 years old primary school teacher at Jaipur got married to Dinesh, who had his own business of paints etc. It was an arranged marriage. Both belonged to very well to do and reputed business families.

Rhea shared- "A few days after the marriage, my sister-in-law asked me jokingly- 'Bhabi why do you speak through your nose?' I told her that I speak like that only and just brushed it aside. I did not give much importance to this innocuous query. But how could I know that it was such a serious issue with my in-laws!

"Not much time had passed, Dinesh and I were just coming to know each other after marriage, when my mother-in-law asked- 'Rhea since when do you have this limp in your leg?' I was shocked and hurt, but didn't know how to react and kept quiet. I was pained when at night Dinesh also commented about the limp. I could not control myself and told him that I had no limp. It may be because of my gait that they felt so. I was deeply hurt by the insensitive attitude of Dinesh and his family members."

A few days before Holi, Dinesh asked me if I would like to visit my parents, as he was visiting Jaipur in connection with his business. I was too happy and grabbed the opportunity. Dinesh dropped me at my parent's house but never returned to pick me up. We only received a phone call two days later. Dinesh's mother spoke with my mother and said, 'We have been cheated. You never told us about Rhea's nasal speech and her limping problem.' No explanation worked, as perhaps Dinesh's mother had already made up her mind to give us an ultimatum. Lot of meetings took place, with mediator and without mediator. To save my marriage, I even underwent detailed medical examination, despite finding the exercise demeaning. But, Dinesh and his parents were not satisfied even with my 'normal' reports.

....With the intervention of some well wishers, Dinesh agreed to take me back, but subject to the condition that we will live in a separate accommodation. Although I was totally against living separately, still I accepted that condition as I was advised not to precipitate the matter any further. I was shocked to see the accommodation arranged by Dinesh for our stay. It then became clear to me that

Dinesh had no intention of living with me. He had actually agreed to bring me back as he could not withstand our 'Jain Samaj's' pressure any further. He had put this condition of separate stay with an ulterior motive; he had intentionally arranged for an accommodation, which was totally unfit for our stay, just to make it impossible for me to stay there; he manipulated the affairs in a manner that he gets an opportunity to say that I have chosen not to stay with him.

I could feel that there was no relationship left between us. Despite all that, I made every effort to put up with Dinesh. I stayed with him even in that inhabitable accommodation, as I did not want to disappoint my parents, who had brought about our reunion after great efforts.

But how long could I continue like this? There need to be two souls to make a marriage work. Dinesh was simply putting up pretence. He would leave home at 8 a.m and would return after 10 p.m. There was hardly any conversation between us despite my efforts. His intentions were clear. I was being put to test. He was testing my patience. How long could I withstand that loneliness? I started feeling depressed.

I ultimately called up my parents. Fortunately, they sensed my condition and I was saved from sinking into serious depression."

Rhea's nasal tone and her slight limp coupled with minor irritants, led to break up of their marriage.

These predicaments are typical to arranged marriages where trust between the spouses and their families their is fragile. The slightest of the issues lead to serious mistrust between the couple, before they have had the time to form a bond. Even if some physical features of the spouse were camouflaged prior to marriage, it is wise not to make an issue out of it, if you have no other problem with your spouse.

We tend to focus more on external features than to appreciate the inner beauty of the spouse. Appearances do matter initially but in the long run, it is the innate strength and beauty, which actually sustains the relationship.

***

- ♥ Material facts and ailment, big or small must be shared before tying the knot, lest it unties the knot causing much pain and grief later on.
- ♥ Being hypersensitive to a minor health condition or revelation about some physical feature of the spouse does not pay; inner beauty is what matters in the long run.

5

CONFLICTS CAN BE CONQUERED

All in a Life Time: Conflicts are Normal

Conflicts and human existence go hand in hand. The best of behaviour does not guarantee perpetual bliss. Fights and conflicts would always be there; they are inevitable and are part of growing up together. Conflicts will always exist and as they do, it is best to patch up quickly lest they turn nasty.

Life is flawed. You want one thing, you get something else. You cannot have sustained happiness. Understanding that conflicts exist in every human association including marriage, makes life easier.

Disagreements in marriage are normal and are rather signs of a healthy marriage. Realising that disagreements indicate that communication is open and that indifference is dangerous, can help change the attitude and approach to handle this relationship.

While conflicts may exist in any association, success of that association requires that conflicts are resolved in a manner which does not hurt either party.

Be yourself

Trying to please others all the time to avoid conflict doesn't help for long. Trying to behave in the manner others want you to, may sap you of your energy and enjoyment in life, because deliberately feigning a posture for too long is absolutely unnatural. Be what you are. Confront the conflict and find ways to resolve it.

Managing the conflicts

It is impossible to go through life without trials and tribulations. They come when you least expect them. They come when you are happily poised; they catch you unaware. Isn't that life?

Experience tells that it is not the people who are passionately in love and more committed that stay married for long, but it is the people who have developed the art and ability to negotiate the disagreements that crop up in day to day life.

We can never be in complete control of what happens in the external world around us, but our internal world is in our hands. We can allow it to be ugly or choose to make it beautiful. Every situation that comes our way is not custom-made to fit our present frame of mind. If every circumstance were to our liking, there would have been no scope for discontentment or conflict; internal growth and transformation would never take place; our life would become stagnant. To handle the changes in our external world, we need to work on our adaptability quotient. It is our own perception that decides our adaptability quotient. Life will always pose challenges; it is up to us how we deal with them to make it joyous. When you flow like a river reveling in every moment of living, you would be able to deal with conflicts on your own.

Couples embroiled in conflicts, taught me great lessons of life. I realised that I myself was using techniques I wished spouses could use to mend their strained relations. I began to manage conflicts in my own life in a better manner. I learnt to make adjustments with ease. Not only that, my husband with whom I had been sharing such stories also adjusted better to my temperament over a period of time and I, to some of his idiosyncrasies. My husband has come to accept my imperfections and I, in turn have become more appreciative of his tolerance.

As the differences and disagreements between spouses over lifestyle, sex, religion, parenting et al, get unfolded over a period of time, they need to manage them skilfully. Differences can't be wiped out as both the spouses have been brought up differently. Managing conflict requires understanding the other's point of view and negotiating differences skillfully.

In life, you cannot find a person with whom you would have no disagreement at all. You still associate and gel great with few. In marriage also, you don't have to find the perfect mate – someone with whom you have everything in common and with whom you would never disagree. Marriage is two individuals coming together who will perpetually disagree; if you learn how to manage disagreements and not avoid them, you can have a great marriage – one that will last. Getting out of the relationship at the smallest of disagreements does not make anyone happy. Because you may not ever find someone, who matches your views and choices. Such break ups also play havoc with children's lives. One has to take a long term view of life.

Sugandhā lost fragrance

Sugandhā belonged to a middle class family. She was born and brought up in Delhi and was accustomed to the ways of metro life. Sunil belonged to an agricultural family of Punjab. His family had shifted to Delhi about 3 years back. Sunil had recently established his business of auto parts in Delhi. Sunil was rustic, coarse and the only culture he was exposed to was agriculture. Sunil could hardly complete a sentence without a relational abuse. Stark differences in their upbringing and backgrounds were the major reason of friction between Sunil and Sugandhā. It made the task of mutual adjustment very difficult. Sunil and his parents had absolutely different ways of handling each situation, right from Sugandhā's ailments to phone calls of Sugandhā's parents.

"After the birth of my son, bleeding continued for more than 15 days; all of a sudden, it became very heavy; I was even unable to stand. I told my mother-in-law about it and requested her to take me to some doctor or my gynaecologist. "This is very natural. Take Isabgol, you will be alright," she advised. Till then, I did not even know what Isabgol was! I was in bad shape when Sunil returned home at about 10 o'clock in the night. He also did not pay much attention to my problem and simply asked me to take rest; he did not even bother that I had been looking after the child all by myself. As if that was not enough, he told me that he had to leave for Chandigarh early morning in connection with his business. I was shattered by the indifferent attitude of Sunil and his mother. Sunil magnanimously told me not to worry as his mother was home, despite knowing fully-well how much his mother really helped me in daily chores. I had no option but to call up my parents next morning.... but a big issue was made out of it ... even otherwise my parents' phone calls were frowned upon not only by my in-laws but also by Sunil... Sunil and his parents did not like my parents visiting even once in a while... Sunil would not even give me pocket money despite my asking and when my parents on their visit gave me some money that too was blown out of proportion..."

Sunil and Sugandhā's distinct background was the root cause of all the conflicts between them. In an orthodox rural Punjabi family, the women never talk about their own discomforts. Even beating at the hands of the husband, once in a while is considered a way of life. An abusive way of talking is considered an attribute of manhood. All this came as a shock to Sugandhā who was a pampered child, being the youngest in the family.

Sunil, during counselling assured that he would not use abusive language in future. He also agreed to give some pocket money to Sugandhā. But he was adamant that Sugandhā's parents should not call her up nor would Sugandhā call them up more than once in a week, as Sunil felt that Sugandhā shared everything that happened at the matrimonial home, with her parents and that her parents were responsible for instigating Sugandhā. "He can't stop us from calling up our daughter; nor would my daughter agree to any such condition," butted in Sugandhā's father, who was present during counselling. "He cannot dictate terms like this. Had Sugandhā not called me up that day, she would have collapsed due to severe anaemia. She has survived because of our intervention, I cannot lose my daughter. If he is serious about his marriage, he should not insist on such conditions," declared Sugandhā's father.

Counselling could not bring them together. Neither side was ready to tactfully manage the conflict. Rather, the conflict got aggravated because of strong and hurting words used by both the sides.

Attitudinal change

Management of conflict demands change in attitude. Realisation that persistent conflicts between parents affect children the most, can bring about change in attitude of the parents. One must realise that in case of separation, even if the custody is shared by both the parents, still children lose out on togetherness and affection of grandparents and other relatives on both the sides.

Single parents who have gone through all this were candid enough to admit this. Ravi shared, "I admit that it was I who decided to part ways. I took a conscious decision as there was no change in Savi's attitude.... I realised that it was getting very tough for Vicky, who was being caught up in our everyday squabbles. I know Vicky would be missing his mother.... I have decided to be a single parent, despite pressure from various quarters to bring a new mother for Vicky....any conflict in the new relationship might be a little too much for him...People caught in similar situations should think twice before running into second marriage. Children don't accept the new partner that easily, which may add to your problems instead of solving them."

Change in attitude can work wonders. Amy Sutherland, who shared her story with the New York Times[1], said, "I wanted – needed to nudge my husband a little closer to perfect, to make him into a mate who might annoy me a little less, who wouldn't keep me waiting at restaurants, a mate who would be easier to love. So, like many wives before me, I ignored a library of advise books and set about improving him. By nagging of course, that only made his behaviour worse.

We went to a counselor. She didn't understand what we were doing there and complimented us repeatedly on how well we communicated. I gave up.

Then something magical happened. For a book I was writing about a school for exotic animal trainers, I started commuting from Maine to California, where I spent my days watching students do the seemingly impossible: teaching hyenas to pirouette on command, cougars to offer their paws for a nail clipping, and baboons to skate board. I listened, rapt, as professional trainers taught dolphins to flip and elephants to paint." Amy Shares, "Eventually it hit me that the same techniques might work on that stubborn but lovable species, the American husband.

The central lesson I learned is that I should reward behaviour I like and ignore behavior I don't. After all, you don't get a seal lion to balance a ball on the end of its nose by nagging.

As I washed dishes at the kitchen sink, my husband paces behind me. 'Have you seen my keys?' He snarls, then stomps from the room with our dog, Dixie, at his heels. In the past I, would have been right behind Dixie. I would have turned off the tap and joined the hunt. But that only made him angrier, and a simple case of missing keys soon would become a full-blown angst-ridden drama starring the two of us and our poor nervous dog.

Now, I focus on the wet dish. I don't turn around. I don't say a word. I'm using a technique I learned from a dolphin trainer.

I love my husband. He's well read, adventurous and does a hysterical rendition of a northern Vermont accent that still cracks me up after 12 years of marriage. But he also tends to be forgetful, and is often tardy and mercurial. He hovers around in the kitchen asking if I read this or that piece in The New Yorker, when I'm trying to concentrate on the simmering pans. He leaves wadded tissues in his wake. He suffers from serious bouts of spousal deafness, but never fails to hear me when I mutter to myself on the other side of the house.

These minor annoyances are not the stuff of separation and divorce, but in sum they began to dull my love for Scott.

I began thanking Scott if he threw one dirty shirt into the hamper. If he threw in two, I'd kiss him. Meanwhile, I would step over soiled clothes on the floor without one sharp word. As he basked in my appreciation, the piles became smaller.

I was using what trainers call "approximations." Rewarding the small steps towards learning a whole new behaviour. You can't expect a baboon to learn to flip on command in one session.

I also began to analyse my husband the way a trainer considers an exotic animal. Enlightened trainers learn all they can about a species, from anatomy to social structure, to understand how it thinks, what comes easily to it and what doesn't.

The exotic animal known as Scott is a loner, but an alpha male. So hierarchy matters, but being in a group doesn't so much. He had the balance of a gymnast, but moves slowly, especially when getting dressed. Skiing comes naturally, but being on time does not. He is an omnivore, and what a trainer would call food-driven.

Once I started thinking this way, I couldn't stop. At the school, I'd be scribbling notes on how to walk an emu, but I'd be thinking, 'I can't wait to try this on Scott.' On a field trip, I listened to a trainer describe how he had taught African crested crane to stop landing on his head and shoulders. He did this by training the birds to land on mats on the ground. This, he explained, is what is called an "incompatible behaviour" a behaviour that would make the undesirable behaviour impossible. The birds couldn't alight on the mats and his head simultaneously.

At home, I came up with incompatible behaviours for Scott to keep him from crowding me while I cooked. I piled up parsley to chop or cheese for him to grate at the other end of the kitchen. Or, I'd set out a bowl of chips and salsa across the room. Soon I'd done it: no more Scott hovering around me while I cooked.

In Sea World San Diego, a dolphin trainer introduced me to least reinforcing syndrome (LRS). When a dolphin does something wrong, the trainer doesn't respond. He stands still for a few beats, careful not to look at the dolphin and then returns to work. The idea is that any response, positive or negative, fuels a behaviour. If a behaviour provokes no response, it dies away. In the margins of my notes I wrote, 'Try on Scott!'

It was only a matter of time, before he was again tearing around the house searching for his keys, at which point I said nothing and kept at what I was doing. It took a lot of discipline to maintain my calm, but results were immediate and stunning. His temper fell far shy of the usual pitch and then waned like a fast-moving storm. I felt, as if I should throw him a mackerel.

After two years of exotic animal training, my marriage is far smoother, my husband much easier to love. Thinking of my husband as an exotic species gave me the distance I needed to consider our differences more objectively. I adopted the trainers' motto: 'It's never the animal's fault.'

Professionals talk of animals that understand training so well they eventually use it back on the trainer. My animal did the same. When the training techniques worked so beautifully, I couldn't resist telling my husband what I was up to. He wasn't offended, just amused. And he soaked it up. For more than I realized.

Last fall, I learnt that I needed braces. They were not only humiliating, but also excruciating. One morning, as I launched into yet another tirade about how uncomfortable I was, Scott just looked at me blankly. He didn't acknowledge my rant in any way, not even with a nod. I quickly ran out of steam and started to walk away. Then, I realised what was happening and asked, 'Are you giving me an LRS?' He was silent. 'You are, aren't you?' He finally smiled, but his LRS has already done the trick. He'd begun to train me, the American wife."

Once you decide that marriage has to work, the clarity of thought with some attitudinal change thrown in, can work wonders.

Watch your thoughts

We all have internal conversation with ourselves, all the time. Since it shapes our outlook, we ought to be careful about the language we use. Words like "terrible" and "horrible" are catastrophic. If we use them, we're bound to spend time dwelling on the negative. Even our thoughts should focus on finding solutions. Be positive. Give it a try; the results would speak for themselves.

Talk it out

It is possible to turn around a relationship, if you get through the resentment by talking it over and by learning about each other's different needs. Communication works wonders.

Signals travelling both ways will surely meet at some wavelength. So, keep the communication on. To keep the marriage happy and happening, one has to be communicative and understanding.

If communication is a problem, one can seek external help. Let someone else do the talking for you.

Counselling: Seeking help in time

When faced with a challenge, climb out of the rally to conquer the mountaintop with the help of a treasured friend, a positive companion.

When she first entered my chamber for counselling, Neelimā looked strikingly laid back, giving little hint of what roiled within. A little cajoling led to the eruption of a volcano; an unending stream of tears rolled down her cheeks, like molten lava.

She shared, "I was very impressed with Rohan's charm and intelligence. Everyone in his family doted on him; he has the gift of making people see themselves in him and offers an enigmatic smile.... I was in heaven. But how was I to know that life is not made only of dreamy stuff.

My daughter was hardly an year old, when Rohan got posted to Muscat to oversee some building project. I would get long poetical letters from him. Then I received a letter, where he mentioned that he suspected that someone was shadowing him; he apprehended danger to his life. It scared me no ends. But I could not discuss this with any of the family members, as he had warned me not to do that. Anyhow, the tense period ended when he returned to India.

I was at my wits end when Rohan told me that he felt that someone was still following him; he would not sleep for days; perpetual anxiety and insomnia took its toll. We went to Rohan's family physician, who advised me to take Rohan to a Psychiatrist, without losing any further time.... With the passage of time and after few visits to the doctor, the heart-breaking revelation was made that Rohan suffered from Schizophrenia. It took some time for enormity of his health problem to sink in.... I could not and did not discuss Rohan's mental state with any of my family members including my in-laws; not even with my brother-in-law, who was staying with us, for fear of Rohan being labelled as "insane"; I would even hide Rohan's medicines. Things went on like this for 4-5 years. Sometimes,

Rohan would be at the best of his brilliance and sometimes, he would sink into depression. Still, I did not discuss about his mental health with any of my friends or family members.

A call from Rohan's boss one afternoon left me shell shocked. He told me tersely that either Rohan puts in his papers or he would be sacked. Rohan had messed up construction of a swimming pool at a leading club in Delhi, which was constructed under his supervision. The pool lacked proper depth and was not even properly levelled.

Where was the option? I got Rohan's resignation letter typed and signed and submitted to his employer, a leading construction company.

...Things were getting worse with each passing day. Rohan was developing a violent streak. One fine morning, not finding his trousers on the hook of the bedroom door, Rohan hit me hard on my head screaming, "I know you are also after my life... you have given the trouser for "Jādu tonā". I thought only Rajiv Gandhi has put plainclothes policemen to shadow me everywhere. But now I know that you are also a party....." I was at my wits end. I was enraged by this sudden attack, but also felt pity for Rohan all the same, who I felt was not in his senses.... time moved slowly. But how long could have I handled him on my own.

My daughter got thoroughly scared, when Rohan hit me in her presence once. Rohan was furious, when he saw me talking to my neighbour's husband. The moment I pulled the door shut, he asked me, 'since when I was flirting with him.' He slapped me hard before I could open my mouth to say anything.... It was getting difficult even to give him medicine. I was finding it impossible to hide Rohan's ailment any further.

I felt awkward when my mother asked me if something was wrong between two of us. Despite my entreaties, my daughter perhaps had told my mother about Rohan slapping me. I felt relieved on finding that my mother did not suspect anything about Rohan's mental health.

It was Holi. My mother and my younger sister came visiting. The fact that Rohan was not at home was a big relief. We were sitting and chatting when Rohan hurriedly returned muttering, "Today they have seen our house. We will have to shift from here, otherwise I would be dead in no time." My mother innocently asked, what was wrong? "You don't know. Mrs. Gandhi's henchmen are shadowing me. She wants me wiped out at any cost," told Rohan. My mother looked askance.

I took Rohan upstairs, persuaded him to take Valium and his other medicines. My mother could however, sense that all was not well.

I was ultimately compelled by my daughter to shift to my mother's house, when Rohan's beatings became more unpredictable, intense and threatening.

I was torn between my daughter and my husband. With no end to these miseries in sight, I myself started sinking into depression. My living with Rohan was getting impossible, as he started suspecting that I was also part of the conspiracy to kill him.

Now I think in retrospect, May be I was not capable of handling his ailment all alone; may be, had I shared Rohan's health problem with his family members, they could provide some clue about his medical history, if any; I might have saved him from getting sucked into it and myself from sinking into depression, had I sought help of my friends, family members or a professional counsellor in the beginning itself.

After three years of separation and having undergone this pain of managing my own depression, I don't think, I can join Rohan again. I am not confident that I won't slip into depression again in his company."

Many people feel "self respect" means never asking for help. It's worth taking an "obligation" if it can save your marriage. Celebrities, persons from corporate world, sports persons normally hire "life coaches" and "personal trainers" to help them improve and overcome their problems and to help them attain their goals.

Nothing shameful in seeking professional help

At first sight, Ridhimā and Sunil looked like a perfect match. But I could feel a rift between the two when I met her in a get-together. Ridhima on much coaxing told, "He can't get over my college fling, which is long dead. Yesterday, I got a call from my colleague. He wanted to brief me about some important official matter. It must have taken me a little more than half an hour on phone. He screamed at me the moment I disconnected the phone- 'You better share your stories while in office; you have no time for me or for kids, even when you are at home.'

"I got furious and could not contain myself and gave him back," told Ridhima ."Since that day, I haven't felt like talking with him. Nor has he cared to say sorry."

She shut me up the moment I offered to help. "You better not. He will then blame me for maligning him even amongst my friends. Once, I had shared my problem with my sister-in-law, who then tried to explain a thing or two to Sunil. Later, I had to bear the brunt on that score. Sunil felt so offended that he warned me never to do that again. Since then, I don't discuss our affairs with any of my friends or with relations, his or mine. But this time, incommunicado has extended little longer..... I am fed up. I can't take it anymore."

Ridhima said, "The problem lies with his psyche, probably because of his parents' troubled relationship. I guess his mother's alleged alliance with his father's friend, left a deep scar on his mind. But I can't be penalised for all that."

My insistence that a counsellor can help Sunil address his psychological problem and bridge the gap between the two without resorting to rhetoric of fault finding, left Ridhima seemingly with a nagging sense that I am making things sound too simple.

If communication is becoming a problem between you and your spouse, there is no harm in seeking intervention of a trusted family member, a common friend, a mature colleague or a well-wisher. It could be anyone who can play a positive role. But, don't forget your spouse's sensitivities and allergy to a particular person.

Where things appear to have gone beyond the well wishers or family members or you apprehend bias, prejudice or have a doubt that confidentiality may not be maintained, it would be best to seek assistance of a professional.

No one is right or wrong. Each spouse has his own perception of reality and may not be able to see the reality of the other. Intervention by a third party helps. A friend, relative or counsellor, who is not part of the spouses' reality, can get an overview of the situation which may be closest to the truth – and yet, not really the truth. For, who knows what the truth really is?

Einstein's theory of relativity holds equally good for a marital relationship. The very concept of time is perceptual and relative, as per Einstein's theory; there cannot be a single reality; there is no such thing as a conclusive reality. All reality is nothing but a figment of our imagination. There are individual perceptions and general perceptions. When lots of people believe the same thing, it has a greater chance of being considered real, and yet it is still just a perception.[2]

The same holds good for spouses' view points; they may think very differently in each situation and both of them may think that they are right, as both have their own reality.

We perceive what our mind wishes to believe. As Hamlet said, "For there is nothing either good or bad but thinking makes it so." A counsellor helps in taking a detached and distant view of things. He helps spouses understand that there is nothing like a "perfect match" ; it is only a mirage ; there is no one who would have everything in common with you and would never disagree with you. A counsellor helps seeing objectively the other side of the picture. A counsellor can assist in resolving disagreements not by removing them but by guiding how to manage them. A little change in attitude would make this relationship a celebration.

Neera and Shantanu, both professionals, decided to go in for a child. Neera quit her job and took up the responsibility of bringing up the child. Immediately thereafter, a power struggle over money emerged. Neera felt she could continue being equally powerful as in the past, whereas, Shantanu felt that he was the sole breadwinner, so he was the boss. There ended the fairy tale. It was a feeling of misplaced entitlement of each of them, which led to a sad state of affairs. This tussle left them insensitive towards each other. Neera was drowned in the child's care and Shantanu in his business. They started feeling a vacuum in their relationship despite there being no apparent issue between the two. They would often pick up fights for no significant reasons. Even their joint efforts, could not help them understand the real issue between them.

They sought the help of a renowned counsellor. The counsellor made them sit together and tried to analyse the real problem. He also spoke with them individually.

The counsellor reached the conclusion that the real cause of all the bickering between the two was the "money issue", which was bringing along with it, other problems. Neera felt that she was capable of earning much more than Shantanu did and had quit the job for family's sake. She expected appreciation on that count. Shantanu on the other hand felt that he was the provider and Neera should realise that. Neera did not feel like asking for money from Shantanu and thought that Shantanu should take care of all her comforts, as before. Economising was beyond her. She failed to realise the fact that they had only one salary now.

Both were provoked by the counsellor to compare their feelings of entitlement to their previous level of material expectations. They were also made to realise how they should be living now, keeping in mind the loss of one salary.

Here comes the role of a counsellor, dealing not only with emotions but also with very mundane and material problems which subtly strike at the root of matrimony.

Change: The key word

While getting into matrimony, both the spouses should expect that certain changes would have to be embraced. But people are terrified of "change" and make utmost efforts to resist it instead of welcoming and attempting to adjust. Change is the fuel of life and is inevitable. But one should not try to change the other.

"If you want your spouse to listen and pay strict attention to every word you say, talk in your sleep."

Marx Groucho

One has to learn to accept the partner as he or she is. A little restraint, not to impose on the other one's own notions of what is right or wrong, goes a long way.

Till the end, generally, we all want a few things about our spouses to change. But, what is different about this desire in those who swim together is the realism that he/ she may never change. And that's okay. Over the years, the edges get softened, like that of pointed pebbles on the shore by the flowing river. Acceptance for each other grows; both surrender to each other in many ways.

If at all one wishes the spouse to change, the best way is to inspire the spouse to change by encouraging him/ her and highlighting his/ her strengths and not by constantly referring to his/ her weaknesses.

The need for compromise is one of the foremost things to accept in a marriage. Many people consider any compromise as a "sell-out", a surrender of values and principles. This is rarely the case. To refuse to adjust one's personality to the expectations of another is pure egotism.

To have a harmonious relationship, one has to ask oneself, "What can I do for the relationship? Do I need to change myself?"

Cannot gel

I often heard people say, "We don't connect; there is absolute incompatibility." Partners do have compatibility issues sometimes. But such cases of intrinsic incompatibility are very few. If someone were to work out the actual percentage of absolutely incompatible couples, I think it would not be more than 2-3 cases out of hundreds. What is generally perceived as incompatibility, is actually the difference in personalities, the different traits and lifestyles of two persons. It is not as if those two persons can't make a couple; an effort has to be made to appreciate and respect the uniqueness of the partner, his/ her tastes and way of life and not to change the other. We have to be respectful to our partner's right to grow in his/ her own way at his/ her own pace; everyone makes his or her own mistakes. Respecting each others' way of life and working together brings harmony. Initial hiccups, if handled tactfully and gracefully, may make a beautiful married life.

By closely observing the spouses in different age groups, I found that later life in marriage is the happiest. That is actually the honeymoon period. It is not when you are trying to find out the ways of the stranger you have started living with or raising small children. It is only later when you look back, your children have grown up – your responsibilities are over– you feel you have done a good job together.

One of my neighbours, Mrs. & Mr. Malhotra are a fine example. They have five children- three sons and two daughters. Mrs. Malhotra was a school teacher and Mr. Malhotra was a gazetted officer in the Ministry of Information and Broadcasting. Mrs. Malhotra, is a simple lady, a contented person and totally devoted to her children and husband. I saw her working round the clock, managing five kids, managing the household, meeting social obligations et al. Mr. Malhotra, hardly bothered about any of these responsibilities. After a few years, Mr. Malhotra resigned from the Government job and plunged into politics. He was hardly available to the family. This added further to Mrs. Malhotra's responsibilities. She had an added responsibility of attending to Mr. Malhotra's visitors at odd hours. She also faced a financial crunch, due to stoppage of inflow of regular monthly income of Mr. Malhotra. To top it all, Mr. Malhotra did not succeed in politics.

We could sense friction between Mrs. and Mr. Malhotra. But we never found her ever cribbing, complaining or even talking about it to anyone; she handled everything so gracefully.

Mrs. and Mr. Malhotra were hardly seen spending any time together. Though married to each other, both had their own worlds. Mrs. Malhotra's universe was her job and the house and nothing beyond. Mr. Malhotra was always involved in his own field away from home. We always wondered, what keeps them together.

Now all their children are married and settled, having their own small worlds. Mrs. Malhotra has retired. Mr. Malhotra more settled in his first calling, which he discovered later in life i.e. reading and literary writing. Mrs. Malhotra also is a voracious reader. We now see them spending beautiful time together; Mr. Malhotra helping Mrs. Malhotra in household work; Mrs. Malhotra tending to Mr.

Malhotra like a child; both pursuing their individual hobbies and also their joint interests , travelling together to different parts of the country. They are now a picture of a "made for each other" couple.

Accepting each other and adjusting to each other's ways paid off.

Acceptance of reality makes life easier

Marriage is a tough life situation. But when we decide to stay married no matter what happens, our attitude towards our spouse changes. We feel relaxed and our behaviour improves.

In Hindus, after completing the seventh step (saptapadi) the bridegroom says, "With seven steps we have become friends (sakhā). May I attain to friendship with thee, May I not be separated from thy friendship". Shatapatha Brāhmana speaks of the wife as the half of one's self – Ardho ha vȧ esha ātmano.

As per religious texts, Hindu husband and wife get united for life in religious ceremonies and likewise in rewards for acts of spiritual merit- Pānigrahanādhi sahatvan karmasu, tathā punyaphaleshucha.

To maintain this life long relationship, imperfections of the spouse need to be endured. In a relationship which begins with a religious ground rule that spouses shall remain united for lifetime, the adjustment becomes easier.

> "Deciding you are never really going to leave, but that you are going to agree to disagree," as Diane Sollee suggests, makes the bad times far easier to endure. We know if we swing with it, we're in a movement that is going to take us somewhere else, and it's a somewhere better. Fights, even worst of them, do not last. My arguments with Chuck have gotten shorter and less hostile over time. We actually end up laughing at some point when the bickering becomes absurd. I know what words hurt him the most, and more and more, I'm thinking them rather than saying them...
>
> When I fight with Chuck, I say I'm sorry as quickly as I can so as not to allow the nastiness to ruin the day. I accept, and expect, feelings of hate to be part of marriage. I am learning how to demonstrate rage silently, to swing

> with it, because I can count on the hate changing into something wonderful. Just like, I can count on tender love turning into bad ass fighting.
>
> It's no longer- if you do that I'm going to leave; it's- you can't do that anymore because we are staying together and that behaviour is not acceptable. You are lucky if that behaviour stops. But if you are like most married persons, no one really changes that much and the only difference in the relationship is that you start tolerating what you used to find intolerable. What happens is we begin to surrender, and this surrender is not a defeat, it's a victory."
>
> *Iris Krasnow*

Acceptance of the fact that no relationship is perfect; and that every association calls for adjustment, makes it easier to live the relationship called marriage.

Marriages of different people work well for different reasons. But all these relationships are woven around the strands of love, friendship, sexual fulfilment, nurture, protection, emotional security, economic responsibility and co-operating. Patterns and the fabric of each marriage vary. It contrasts sharply with others. But the common thread which runs through all these relationships is that each of the spouses believes in the continuity of a long term partnership.

Count your blessings

Marriage requires making frequent stops to count the blessings of this moment, this day and of the days gone by. Burden of relationship may weigh you down, sometimes you may want to break free. But comparing your relationship with someone else's marriage, which is not doing too well, may make you realise that you are much better off. Trivia can be managed.

It might amaze you to see someone close to you, being stuck together throughout their life, despite an imperfect relationship. But you will find that they have perfectly come to live with each other's faults and need each other and both acknowledge this fact.

Marriage is an acquired relationship which can be lived, as we live through all other relationships.

You cannot measure your own relationship on someone else's scale.

Divorce: Not a panacea

Divorce is not a pill which you take and everything will be all right. Divorce is not the remedy for all your miseries. Hindu law, strictly speaking, did not allow divorce, except in certain communities under certain circumstances. In lower social strata it was permitted by custom. Though some of the smritikārs did not deal with divorce in the sense it is now understood, but they did declare that a woman could take a second husband in certain circumstances. The Manusmriti mentions :

नष्टे मृते प्रव्रजिते क्लीवे च पतिते पतिः ।
पंचसु आपत् सु नारीणां पतिः अन्यो विधियते ।।

Naste mrite pravrajite klive cha patite patih;
Panchsu āpat su nārinām patih anyoh vidhiyate.

(If a husband absconds or deserts his wife, dies, becomes ascetic, is impotent or dissolute, the wife is free to have another husband.) Re-marriage of women are permitted by the Scriptures under these five peculiar circumstances.

There was a deep-rooted sentiment against any provision for divorce in the legislation, which was being forged after independence of India.

Evidence was placed before the Hindu Law Committee that there were thousands of cases of desertion of women by their husbands and many cases were brought to its notice in which remarriage had been desired and was possible, but could not be effected due to the then existing law against divorce; it was also placed before the committee that the grounds other than desertion also required serious consideration. The committee after considering the material, made a strong report in favour of the proposed legislation providing relief by way of divorce in appropriate cases. The recommendations in the report of the Rau Committee on the questions of marriage and divorce were substantially accepted by the Parliament. The concept of breaking of marriage was brought in to meet extreme situations. Divorce was contemplated, as an exception to be resorted to in exceptional circumstances.

We have however, travelled a long way. With change in the social milieu, the definition of "exceptional circumstances" has undergone a sea change.

There is no denying the fact that things are much different today. More and more situations may demand separation. But, it is no less important to understand that marriage is not a pathological condition, which gets cured with the potion of divorce or a new relationship.

Marriage is a relationship. If you aren't good at relationships, divorce and remarriage is no guarantee of perpetual bliss ever after. The sense of freedom and relief is short-lived.

The fact that children suffer the most in the case of break up, should not be lost sight of. Breakup can prove devastating for children. It may leave them unsure of their own relationships; the lasting trauma amongst children of broken homes may leave them apprehensive about failure of their own marriage.

Once we choose to have children, we have to make every effort to make the relationship last.

It may be a good idea to spend energy to make your marriage work, as harmony at home brings joy and peace in society. You realise that the thoughtful journey you make, helps making this world a beautiful place for all, especially the next generation.

But clinging on to a relationship which is dead, just because of social pressure or to avoid social stigma, is no good.

Good bye can be said

Divorce is a remedy of last resort. But it can surely be resorted to when the relationship turns hostile and is proving disastrous to the health of spouses.

Alaknandā must have been around 32 years of age and Shirish 36 years old. They had eight years old daughter. Shirish had filed a petition for divorce on the ground of cruelty.

No amount of counselling could persuade Shirish to join Alaknanda. Nor could Alaknanda be convinced to let go of the relationship. Both had their own reasons for "fighting free of" and "clinging on to" the relationship.

One day, during counselling, Shirish acted strange; he suddenly got up from the chair and started enacting how he was being shadowed by a strongman with pistol hidden under his shirt, which seemed imaginary to me. He told, "Alaknanda's father is after my life. He even sent a muscle man to my office to liquidate me. I was fortunate that I was in my boss's cabin at that time and could not be traced".

I could sense a schizophrenic streak in Shirish. Schizophrenic disorders are generally characterised by a distortion in thinking and perception; reportedly, a schizophrenic patient suffers from delusions and sometimes feels that some natural or unnatural forces are at work to influence his/ her thoughts and life. The schizophrenic often sees himself as the centre of all that happens; hallucinations are quite common. Shirish kept a safe distance from Alaknanda and her father in the court room also; he was always accompanied by his father. With each passing date of hearing, Shirish's mental health was deteriorating; his facial expressions, demeanour and gait easily gave away his delicate mental equilibrium. I could feel that Alaknanda's mere presence put Shirish to extreme discomfort. The fact that Shirish was getting sucked into the quicksand of emotional turmoil was too obvious to be missed.

Where was the question of Shirish agreeing to join Alaknanda, when Alaknanda's very presence made Shirish so restless. Efforts to make Alaknanda see the reality bore no fruit. Alaknanda rather reacted, "I cannot accept divorce even in my dreams. In our community there cannot be any divorce; girl is married only once.... she leaves her husband's home only after death.... and no other way....". She refused to accept that she was torturing Shirish by her mere insistence to join his company. Shirish's mental health was on a constant decline. Death of Shirish's constant companion/ his father during the divorce proceedings, only made the matter worse.

During counselling, advocates from both the sides fairly agreed that there was no possibility of Alaknanda and Shirish living together.

But, Alaknanda's advocate expressed his helplessness and inability to bring about Alaknanda to accept this stark reality.

Shirish had even stopped paying maintenance to Alaknanda and his advocate informed that Shirish had stopped going to work. Then suddenly, Shirish who was otherwise very regular in attending the court proceedings stopped appearing. Shirish's advocate revealed that he was admitted to Institute of Human Behaviour & Allied Sciences, Dilshad Garden in Shahdara, Delhi.

Shirish's mental health took a serious hit, when his desperate efforts to break free from his imaginary tormentor failed.

One may not be at fault, but still sometimes a situation may demand one's pound of flesh. One can't help but pay. The sooner the better. Who knows, had Alaknanda realised timely that no life was left in their relationship and rather she was perceived as a threat to his life by Shirish, he would have been saved from sinking into deep depression and schizophrenia.

Sometimes there is no other way than to let go.

***

- ♥ Conflicts are normal; don't pretend in order to avoid them; be yourself.
- ♥ Differences can be talked out. Take professional help if need be; sooner, the better.
- ♥ Little change in attitude and respect for each other's point of view helps in managing conflict.
- ♥ Acceptance of reality that no one is perfect, makes life easier.
- ♥ When feeling low, count your blessings.
- ♥ You are not perfect and would carry your own imperfections, wherever you go. Therefore, divorce is not a panacea.
- ♥ But goodbye can be said, when relationship feels cold and hostile.
- ♥ Clinging on to dead relationship does not help.

6

ABUSIVE RELATIONSHIPS

Marriage has generally been found to be beneficial for health. Married men and women reportedly live longer than the singles. Married people as a group also have better psychological health than non-married persons, as per a study of 3000 men and women published online in Psychosomatic Medicine, which examined the relationship between marital stress and coronary heart disease or death. But marital disharmony can lead to varied health problems. A 2003 study reported in the journal "Archives of General Psychiatry" showed that after marital spats, blisters generally healed more slowly, a sign that stress interfered with the functioning of immune system. The study also showed that in hostile couples or those who hurled insults or rolled their eyes while arguing, the healing was 60 percent slower than in couples who didn't display antagonistic behaviours. In such couples, women tended to take longer to heal than men.[1]

Dana Crowley Jack, a professor at Western Washington University and author of the 1991 book "Silencing the Self", reportedly said that women's motivations for avoiding conflict are complex. Women are socialised to keep feelings of conflict with their spouses to themselves, believing that their behaviour will protect their marriages or family relationship. One way of being pleasing is to go along with what the other person wants and to ignore your own desires, likes and dislikes.[2] But, this can lead to immense stress and may cause major health problems.

A relationship is destructive, if it feels scary, cold, or unfriendly and you're staying in it because you dream it might change for the better someday or because you think, it is better than being alone. If tension has hardened into contempt, it is better to admit it and move on. Such a relationship isn't better than being alone. Staying married under false pretences or because of pressure to keep up those pretences, is worse than anything else.

Sudhir and Ārushi got married after 5 years of courtship. Both worked for a leading ad-agency at fairly high positions. One day, Sudhir walked into his office with one palm bandaged. He also sported dark shades that he kept on as he got down to work with his one good hand, while cracking jokes with his colleagues.

Behind the good humour however, was a dark tale. During counselling, one of the close friends of Sudhir disclosed, "Sudhir recently had another violent and abusive encounter with Arushi. This is an ordeal that Sudhir suffers frequently. This time Arushi has given him a black eye; at other times, she's used a rolling pin, cricket bats, anything that came her way when she was enraged. Most of her colleagues wouldn't know this aggressive female. At work, Arushi is a normal, regular professional, competent at her job, courteous with co-workers, respectful to her superiors."

Experts blame this behavioural duality on "social fragmentation". The break-up of the joint family, the growth of DINKs, (Double Income No Kids), changing job markets and rising disposable incomes are all redefining new work cultures and therefore, new individuals. What we now have, are individuals with "zero-tolerance levels". Interaction with individuals in different stages of breaking up (of their bond) revealed that cases of individuals exhibiting "unusual" behaviour are on the rise. Under a civilised veneer, urban society is showing an inclination for the bizarre and the unusual. As one progresses and becomes more 'civilised' with education, there is a noticeable disregard for norms binding society. Individual interests start taking precedence.

Walking out of marriage however, makes sense, when the domestic situation becomes emotionally or physically damaging for either of the partners. There are situations in which breaking up is the only solution; physical abuse, mental torture, an alcoholic spouse, consistent extra-marital flings of the spouse, loneliness, dejection, and excessively suspicious spouses are the examples of situations, where it may become imperative to walk out.

"The miserable husband reflected that her lust seemed to fire at the sight of every man but him that she nagged, wheedled for fine clothes to attract strangers, that the first pregnancy meant the decline of her health and the assumption of permanent valetudinarianism."

Germaine Greer in "The Female Eunuch"

In such situations parting ways may be the only solution.

Incompatibility

There are cases where there is nothing grossly wrong with the relationship, still the relationship turns cold. One is not at ease with one's relationship for no obvious reason. Nalini, was a Kashmiri girl and Sumesh belonged to a baniyā family from UP. They were studying together at IIM, Ahmedabad. They shared a great relationship. After their placements, they decided to tie the knot. Although their families were not very comfortable with the alliance, mainly due to cultural differences, they ultimately consented to the marriage.

Within a few months of marriage, Nalini started feeling annihilated. She was not able to pin point during counselling session, as to what was it that made her feel uneasy in the relationship. She could only say, "We simply don't gel. We have fights on anything and everything. We are unable to get along"

In earlier times, issues relating to compatibility and survival were different. Women had not gained confidence. Marriage continued irrespective of what men or women wanted. But today things are different. Women are now deciding for themselves whether to stay in marriage or call it quits.

Lives were simpler earlier ; equations have become very complex today.

Nalini said, 'It is probably his habit of keeping count of everything, his habit of burping loudly, getting into bed with his office clothes on and endless such things... I don't feel like complaining about such petty things but all these things really put me off. He is a nice and simple person. He is a great friend but somehow I have not been able to adjust with him in his avtār as a husband. I can only say that we can't make a couple. We can't be a husband and wife."

This was beyond me initially. Probably Nalini could sense my disbelief. She could perhaps read my thoughts that how could a person seek divorce over such silly things. She preempted me, "We continue to be friends. We have talked about it at length. He understands that we can't be happy as a husband and wife." She kind of assured me.

Sumesh shared, "I do feel very sad about our break up. But what can I do? I could feel that she is not happy in this relationship. It bothered me no end initially. But now, I have come to accept it. I really love her and can't see her sulking. What is the use of putting up pretences, when you don't share the warmth which should be there between husband and wife?"

After the statements of Sumesh and Nalini were recorded for divorce by mutual consent, they were seen sitting on the last bench of the courtroom chatting away to glory. After sometime, I saw Sumesh fetching a washed apple for Nalini. The relief on their faces was apparent. Perhaps, they had rediscovered the warmth of a friendship which had been lost in the bond of matrimony.

It was little strange. But, may be it was best for them to part gracefully, instead of feeling stifled in marriage.

Rachna faced the same predicament

Rachna's predicament was somewhat similar to that of Sumesh. She did not want to break the bond, but there was no other option.

Rachana and Shekhar were childhood friends. Their families were also very close. Both the families had shifted to US and were NRIs. After both Rachana and Shekhar were professionally settled, their parents felt that they made a good match. Although Rachana and Shekhar had not thought about marriage till then, they agreed to their parents' wishes as they knew each other pretty well.

Sometime after their marriage, bickering started between them on absolute non issues. Whether it was buying of grocery from a particular store or Rachana's loud way of reacting to small things, even at public places and several other things like that.

Shekhar during counselling was firm that they could no longer have the same cordiality, which they shared earlier.

Rachana, in an individual session of counselling sobbed inconsolably. "I have been trying to make this marriage work. But I don't know what went wrong and where. I don't deny that on occasions, we have had tough fights". She sought some more time to reflect. But, Shekhar was clear in his mind that their marriage was beyond repair. Still, he agreed to give Rachana sometime to do the rethinking.

On the next date of hearing, Rachana, during 'in-camera' proceedings agreed that perhaps divorce was the only solution. She gave her consent for divorce. But after her consent for divorce was recorded, she was seen crying again. Rachana was informed that she could take her own time to re-think before the divorce was granted by the court. She need not feel pressured having made a statement before the court.

Rachana was called for counselling again to confirm, if there was any pressure on her. "There is no pressure. Our parents have left it to us to decide. Both of us have had numerous sessions. I understand that this relationship is simply not working for us. But my heart does not accept this. My heart sinks at the very thought of break-up. Shekhar had been a great buddy since childhood, but I know we have not been able to live happily," she confided.

After the divorce was granted, Rachana shared, "I feel much lighter now. I cannot say that I am actually happy after divorce. But I think Shekhar was not too happy in the relationship. I could not have kept begging him for some more time to see, if it worked.... I think it is in the best of our interests."

If a relationship feels tense and cold all the time, lacks warmth and smells of indifference, it is all right to call it quits.

Physical violence

When suspicion, constant abuse and physical violence take the place of trust, mutual understanding and love, as happened in the case of Nayanika and her Australian husband Brad, it is time to part ways. Nayanika shared, "It is not easy for anyone to fathom how a life so beautiful could turn out to be horrible, as it did in my case.

"I was in a different country with a person who I thought loved and understood me completely. That was the impression I got when I was dating him.

"I was financially secure and had established my career as a producer, when I met Brad. He was just the man, I always dreamed of. I was so much in love with him that I quit my established career in India to settle down with him in Australia. We got married and settled in Australia.

Initially there was no trouble. But within a month's time, Brad's deep sense of insecurity surfaced. He was pursuing higher studies and was working on weekends. We were mostly living off my savings. My parents also helped me. Yet, he would constantly convey in subtle ways that my parents should be financing us since he was not having a regular job. It seemed to me to be an indirect hint at dowry, and I was very hurt. Not only this, he became extremely possessive of me to the extent that he would not like me talking to anyone, even my own family members. At first, it was just verbal abuse. Later, things came to such a pass that he started physically abusing me. I was completely clueless about how to handle the situation, because no matter what I did to ease things between the two of us, it would invariably backfire. My in-laws tried to help me, but could not do much, though we were living in the same house. In any case, he would not listen to them.

Day in and day out, we went through the same ritual of abuse and hurt. Typically, it used to be one day of having a fight followed by two to three days of remorsefulness from his side, and then back to square one. He would ask for time to mend his ways. That's it. We hardly talked. He would come home and sit before TV and then go to sleep. I gave him his space. However, when I tried to look out for my space by connecting with my friends and family or doing things I loved, he would object.

I was not working then. It was a very painful period, but I never gave up.... Then I got pregnant. I thought with the arrival of the baby, he would be a changed person. But once again I was proved wrong. My lullaby to my baby seemed like noise to him! My mother came to see me and stayed with us. I could not even step out of my room, as he accused me that I was leaving him! Often he would shake my son, Neel, to pacify him. He would say that he was making a man out of him! I explained to him that Neel was only a one-month-old baby!

Things just became worse. One day, in a fit of rage he abused me physically and tried to do the same with my son. That was it. I decided to call it quits.

I was bleeding from my lips. I told Brad, I was leaving. He thought it was a joke. Since he tried to keep me away from others, he thought, even if I tried, nobody was going to help me.... I filed for divorce and got it soon within 2-3 months. He never tried to talk with me, stop or delay divorce proceedings.

Today, I have firmly put my past behind me, as I chart a whole new life. I am back into what I was known best for, "production". I stay with my parents and have great time with them, with my son, my friends and my career. At the same time, I am not against marriage. I may marry again, if I meet my Mr Right."

Probably what Nayanika did was in the interest of all of them, under those circumstances. Cases involving abuse were eye-openers and great lessons of life. It was unbelievable to see decent looking persons unfolding into wild and violent husbands. Not only that, they were unable to handle their violent self, despite much efforts.

Dual personality of ankur – made things worse for Rashmi

Rashmi and Ankur were doing their Ph.D from Delhi University. Long hours in lab brought them closer. They decided to marry. Rashmi was a Bengali and Ankur, a Jat from Haryana. There was a lot of resistance from Ankur's family. Even Rashmi's parents were not very happy about Rashmi marrying a non-Bengali and that too, a Jat. When both of them conveyed that they had already decided to tie the knot, both the families were left with no option but to accept their decision.

Rashmi confided, "I was dumbfounded when he slapped me hard on my cheek. I could not comprehend what had happened? Why did he hit me? My senses were numbed. It was just 10 days after our marriage. This incident took place at the dining table, when he shouted at me, "You can't even roast a papad properly." All I remember is that he had some argument with his mother before coming to dining table. My sister-in-law, simply took me away to my bed room.

I looked askance at her. "You probably want to know as to how I reacted. I did not react at all. I was too shocked to react to something so immense. I did not even cry. I don't know why? I simply kept sitting on my bed like a corpse. He came to the bedroom and sat on the floor next to my feet. He profusely apologised and swore not to behave like that. He kept on caressing me..."

Stone faced, Rashmi narrated many such incidents, which would have torn apart any body's soul.

"I really don't know how I kept on bearing that torture. Of course, initially I myself couldn't understand anything about his violent behaviour. One moment he would hit me and the very next moment he would beg forgiveness. I was totally confused. Moreover, I lacked the courage to discus all that with my sister or my parents, for the fear of their backlash. Once he beat me black and blue. I wore full-sleeves blouses to work to hide the tell-tale signs."

Meanwhile, we had two kids ... such incidents started affecting my kids. Initially, my sister-in-law would help me but she also gave up by and by. Once, in a get together over dinner at our house, he hit me before his own colleagues. On another occasion, he visited my office and called me names, putting me to immense embarrassment. Kavita, my colleague and a friend, who had already sensed that there was something amiss, asked me, what was going on between us. Still, I did not share much with her. I still don't know why did I not share my grief with my most trusted colleague?...

I found my own way of tackling the hopeless situation I was in. To be away from Ankur, I got myself transferred out of Delhi. I did not tell him that the transfer was on my request. I caught up with life in those three years. Those years of chosen separation gave me thinking time. I then decided that this man cannot be believed. I filed for Judicial Separation, being not very sure whether I should be seeking divorce; would that be in the interest of my kids?...

I did not tell anyone in office. Rather, I wanted it to remain a secret. I felt ashamed of the whole affair, although I was not at fault. Ankur was just the same. He visited me, apologised and begged of me, but somewhere, he could sense my firmness this time..."

"I am highly educated. I am also holding a good position in my job, earning sufficient to survive on my own. I could not find any reason, why an educated girl like me could not take this step earlier? Why did I allow myself to be ill treated at Ankur's hands so long? How could I take abuses from him? How could I allow him to trample on my dignity? I am shocked at my own self. What shocks me more is that I am the member of the Official Committee to address sexual harassment complaints of women employees in the organisation, I am working for. I am really at a loss," tears welled in Rashmi's eyes.

Rashmi shared, "On some occasions, he even had the cheek to ask me for sex after the incidents of beatings. But, I had evolved a novel way to withstand his pressure. I would wear a hugging pair of jeans and sleep off," she smiled sheepishly.

"Did you not seek help of any of his family members, friends or well wishers ?" I had asked. Rashmi said, "I didn't even seek help of his friends. Probably, I felt that his friends and colleagues may not even believe me because he looks so decent and cultured. He is a brilliant officer; has earned a good reputation at his workplace. No doubt some of his colleagues with whom he was closely associated, knew that he was volatile in nature. But anyway, that does not bother me anymore. I have taken a separate accommodation and have not joined him on my transfer back to Delhi. He initially tried to play that "forgive me" trick with me. But no, it can't continue. I am pretty much at peace with myself. Rather now I wonder, how I continued with him for so long..."

Ankur did not agree for divorce by mutual consent, despite numerous counselling sessions. He kept on insisting that he was confident that they could live together. He even agreed to give an undertaking that he would not give any reason to Rashmi, to complain. But he did not agree for divorce.

An extreme behaviour like this appears to be akin to a split personality. May be, Ankur actually needed some psychiatric help.

Tehmina's biographical account

Tehmina Durrani in her biographical account in "My Feudal Lord", described her similar experience and termed her marriage to Mustafa Khar, one of the Pakistan's most eminent figures, a nightmare. Tehmina narrates:

"Mustafa was violently possessive and pathologically jealous. One moment, she would be beaten black and blue; another moment he would apologise profusely. But, Mustafa succeeded in cutting her off from the outside world." For fourteen years Tehmina suffered alone, in silence. She has mentioned,

"... I had fallen into the classic trap of the Pakistani woman. The goal is marriage and, once achieved, the future is a life of total subordination. I had no power, no rights, no will of my own,..."

Tehmina narrates, One day he began to interrogate me about my marriage to Anees (my earlier husband). How had we met?... Answer me! He grabbed my right wrist and twisted, forcing me to my knees....

Suddenly he threw me down on to the bed and jumped on me. Sitting astride my belly, he slapped me in the face repeatedly with his open palm, forehand and backhand.... he pulled at my hair, thrusting my head from side to side. Like lightning, he leaped off me. One hand clutched my long, braided hair and jerked me off the bed and on to the floor. He threw me against a wall, picked me up and threw me against another one again, and again, and again. I no longer knew what was happening. Something burst in my ears. I felt an agonising pain in my eyes. Something split. Something swelled. Then the pain merged into one deep, enthralling sense of agony.

I did not know how long the beating lasted. It could have been ten minutes; it could have been two hours. The intensity made it an eternity. Then, quite suddenly, it was over. His fury was sated....

He looked up at me, shattered, transformed from a wild, vengeful beast into a meek and a frightened little child. He fell at my feet and wept. 'I'm sorry! I'm sorry! He wailed."What have I done to you? He begged forgiveness. He said that he must have been possessed by an evil spirit. He had not meant to hurt me. He could not understand his actions; perhaps .. he could not bear the idea of his wife with another man, even if it was a husband.

I was very confused by the unaccountable pity I felt for this man, who had his forehead on my feet, anointing them with his tears. I tried to forgive him, but the pain would not allow me to forget.

... He kept me suppressed and cloistered, but then again he treated me as a companion. He discussed politics with me ....

When he was in a sunny frame of mind, he was loving and considerate. He fed me with his own hands. He dreamt with me. He promised to be a good husband."

Tehmina shares that when she decided to rebel, the price she paid was extremely high; she was deprived of all the financial support; she lost the custody of her four children and found herself alienated from her friends and disowned, even by her parents.

The consequences of walking out of an abusive relationship may not be as bad always. In any case, there is no point clinging on to a wild and violent spouse, as if there would be no life after break-up.

Enduring consistent violence only begets further violence.

Abusive and alcoholic spouse

Anjali quit alcoholic husband

Puneet had filed a petition for restitution of conjugal rights. Anjali refused to join his company. During counselling what Anjali shared was a headlong dash into the crevices of her emotional folds. She said, "I did not want to break my marriage and that is why I tolerated this sick, perverted person for so long. But, I won't tolerate him anymore. I haven't made up my mind yet, to call it quits. But, I can't join him either. There are so many things which I feel ashamed of, even to share with others."

"Puneet would come home drunk or would get drunk at home. Not only this, he would force me to drink and indulge in all sorts of things with him. Puneet would force me to have anal sex. He was least bothered about my discomfort. He would not listen to me and would even compel me to suck his member, though I detested it. On some occasions, he even discharged in my mouth forcibly and would not let me spit. This was becoming his routine..... Things crossed all limits when Puneet didn't even spare Rehan, our 2 years old son. That night I refused to take it anymore. He pulled me with a jerk; Rehan got up as a result of this commotion and started howling. Puneet forced whisky down Rehan's throat to make him quiet and to put him back to sleep."

Anjali confessed that perhaps she should have put her foot down much earlier, but could not muster courage, because of Rehan.

A large percentage of divorce litigation initiated by wives involved allegation of mental and physical torture by alcoholic husbands.

Pārvati refused to take it anymore

Amar ran a small tailoring shop. Parvati was also contributing to the family kitty by working as a part-time maid in a few bungalows.

It was Amar's petition for restitution of conjugal rights. Parvati refused to join Amar's company and shared, "Amar would beat me up at the slightest of pretexts. That was not all, his mother and sister instead of diffusing the situation would also join in.....

That evening my mother-in-law blew a small incident out of proportion.... I generally returned home at about 6 p.m. after finishing my work. My friend Kalawati had cut her hand. I had to accompany her to the nearby doctor, which delayed me a little. It was 7:00 p.m. when I reached home. My mother-in-law started shouting the moment I entered the house. She fumed, "With whom have you been loitering around? Don't you know I take my dinner at 7:00 p.m? Let Amar come today."

Ignoring my mother-in-law's sermon, I went straight into kitchen, cooked and served the dinner to her. After I was done with the kitchen, I went and sat in the courtyard to catch my breath, when Amar hit me from behind. He had hit me so hard that I almost choked. He called me names..... levelled allegations, wanton, imaginary and irresponsible. It was then that I decided– no more of this abuse. I made up my mind that there was no point in spending my life in rancour and drudgery. I would be better off without my cantankerous mother and sister-in-law and drunkard husband. "I cannot think of joining him anymore," Parvati was firm and refused to join Amar's company.

But there are others who could not come to terms with breaking up with alcoholic husbands

Vidya could not come to terms with breaking up

Though Vidya had filed a petition for divorce, but she did not actually want to break up. What Vidya shared surprised me no end. She confided, "I don't mind if Rattan beats me. He is my husband. He can do that if I go wrong somewhere. But my brother-in-law and sister-in-law have no right to act rough with me."

To return to her matrimonial home, Vidya only wanted an assurance from Rattan that his brother and sister would not beat her. She did not really mind Rattan's beatings.

> "I am 39 and have been submitting to corporeal punishment from my husband, ever since we married 15 years ago. We have both treated this matter of punishment, as a normal sort of proceeding. It was not until recently, when we saw some letters in 'Forum' that we realised there were people who had guilt complexes about spanking their mates.
>
> Our ideas are quite simple. My husband happens to believe that in marriage, the husband should be the boss. I agree with him and I recognise that wrong-doing should be punished. We both think that the simplest, most convenient, most effective and most natural way for a man to punish

the faults of his woman is to spank or whip her; but not too severely, certainly not brutally."

Letter in "Forum" Vol.2 No.3 quoted by Germaine Greer in "The Female Eunuch"

Ramya loved Angad but hated his drinking habit

Rāmyā, belonged to upper middle class and was teaching at a Central School in Delhi. Angad, her husband was an officer in the Central Government.

Ramya had filed a suit for judicial separation. She shared during counselling that she did not hate Angad. She hated him when he was drunk. She said, "I am thoroughly fed up with Angad now. Promises were made only to be broken... I gave him an ultimatum. He assured me that he would not give me an opportunity to complain. But one night, when I heard that dreadful screeching of the bike, the sound it used to make when he would park it in a drunken condition, I realised that he was beyond me... The moment I confronted him and reminded him about his promise, he started breaking glasses, throwing plates, turning tables, hitting anything and everything, which came his way in a drunken stupor. Next day, he simply forgot all about it.....

I can't endlessly keep buying crockery and keep getting furniture repaired, besides being sneered at by the neighbours. My growing children are suffering the most. They have stopped going out to play. My children now even shun their friends, as they start singing "Sharabi... sharabi...", the moment my children enter the colony park. They don't say anything to me, but I feel their pain and agony. The younger one is becoming self destructive. He even told me the other day that he would run away, if Papa didn't mend his ways. That scared the life out of me. I have already lost my husband. I can't afford to lose my children."

Conversation with Ramya revealed that in the heart of her hearts, Ramya still did not want to break the marriage. She hoped against the hope that Angad would quit this killer habit someday. She had sought a decree of judicial separation only at that juncture.

Conflicts can and should be overcome for the sake of harmony at home, for the children and a life of togetherness. Yet, going separate ways may be equally essential for the revival of tormented body and soul!

Breaking up is hard, but not as much, as one may think. We overestimate the heart-crushing blow from a split, and some of us make particularly inaccurate forecasts. In the moments following a breakup, life can seem like a cruel joke that will never end but that initial split is not as crushing as expected. Not only that, life snaps back to pre-breakup mode, twice as fast as one would predict.

***

- ♥ Marriage is a beautiful relationship. But one can quit, if it becomes an unending torture.
- ♥ Incompatibility and abusive spouses, could be valid reasons to call it quits.

7

THE RECENT TRENDS

Upward Shift in Marriageable Age

As per the 2007 AC Nielsen survey, 79 percent Indian men and women held the 30s to be the right age for marriage[1]. The age for marriage is on the rise and the duration of marriage is on decline.

Just a few decades back, people got married at a much younger age. Consequently, there was greater flexibility in their attitudes and personalities. Couples grew up and developed belief systems together. It made adjustment much easier as there were fewer fixed ideas and opinions to deal with. With the marriage age moving into late twenties and thirties, the couples who come together have fully developed personalities, fixed likes and dislikes, firm opinions about everything from family to how children should be brought up. Adjustment, between two such well defined personalities, is much more difficult. There is now that much less space for accommodating different viewpoints and different ways of doing things. As a result, the small differences get blown out of proportion, and couples seem to be ready to walk out on each other at the drop of a hat.

The system of joint families and large extended families living in close knit social settings discouraged separation. With the disintegration of the joint family system and rise of nuclear families, the social pressure to make things work has waned, and the pressure valves built into close knit extended families have also disappeared. Earlier, elders had a say and would guide the erring spouse, and would extend a loving hand to the victim spouse.

Even if they were not personally happy in the marriage, women earlier tried to stay on for reasons such as family honour, fear of social stigma, her non acceptability at parents' place after marriage, In case of disappointment, men also did not break-up the marital bond and rather looked for satisfaction outside. Whether that was a good thing or the current trend of break ups is better, is anybody's guess. But it did provide children with both the parents.

Parameters of match making

The trends in match making are changing. There is a shift in focus from physical features to mental compatibility and material comforts. Internet has become a vehicle of social change.

The results of a recent survey[2] revealed the kind of partners, are now sought in the marriage market. It shared the concern of the parents that women are getting very picky about the partners they want. It reported that Kalpana Swamy, a single girl, a busy brand consultant who shifted to Mumbai, recently wrote a three-page letter to her mother which said, "Dear mom, this is to counter the flood of CVs of suitable boys you are sending. It's irritating to read about people who don't excite me," and sent the list of features she was looking for in the spouse. She mentioned that the man in her life needed to respect that she loves her job, his wavelength needs to match; compatibility and chemistry matter the most, was the final caveat.

In yet another case, where the girl had left home only four years ago, the parents shared, "Living alone in Mumbai changed this girl. She does not want a "good boy" from a "good family", with matching caste and horoscope and instead reeled off her priorities: He has to be smart, sensible, sincere, sensitive and qualified enough to lead a better life. She enjoyed her work, so the man in her life needed to respect that. She mentioned that wavelengths need to match. "Compatibility and chemistry matter the most to me," was the caveat, the final warning that these particular things are to be considered before any decision is taken."

Reema's aunt cribbed, "She wants someone who's also working in Bangalore ("I don't want to quit my job for a man."). She wants someone who's more or less her age ("I should be able to relate to him."). She is looking for someone whose salary outshines hers ("I don't want my husband to get an inferiority complex."). She wants someone whose parents live in the same city as hers ("I don't want to split my vacations by shuttling between two cities."). She systematically says "no" to men who don't appeal to her. She doesn't care about caste and horoscope match or the fact that she's 28."

Compatibility is now the code word. Personality profile has overtaken sun signs. Women's empowerment, their economic independence and new outlook about their sexuality have transformed the underpinnings of the arranged marriages. The younger generation is talking about mental compatibility more than matching horoscopes.

The Director, Centre for Social Research, Delhi pointed out that in a study of over 3,000 matrimonial ads between 1967 and 1997, the centre recorded a noticeable shift from an exclusive focus on physical appeal to intellectual and economic merits of girls[3].

Tushar Guha, a psychologist-counsellor with Nrityanjali in Mumbai was quoted by a national fortnightly[4] saying, "The present scenario reflects a confused search for glamour and an attempt at social climbing.... too many young people seem to seek "trophy wife and husband", somebody who looks good, is well-educated and has a sparkling career graph. But scratch below the surface, 60 percent of the youth are still mama's boys or papa's girls. They have just become smarter about choosing their partners."

The collision between modernity and tradition came to the fore in the statistics revealed by a shaadi.com survey. The specifications desired by young boys and girls in their spouses reflected not only the yearning for modernity, but also an unwillingness to undo ties with traditions. Shaadi.com survey reported, "If 64 percent men in Delhi favour inter-caste marriage, 59 percent desire fair women. If 62 percent Mumbai women want to work after marriage, a mere 37 percent are open to inter-caste marriage. In Bangalore, 54 percent prefer working wives, while Pune girls want the big-city life with

88 percent men seeking educated brides, yet only 29 percent want working wives."[5]

The ground reality appears to be that although the younger generation has embraced modernity, they have not yet unshackled themselves from some of the age old parameters of a "good" husband or wife.

Great surge in divorce rate

Marriages have become fragile. Divorce is becoming a common reality. The trend of short lived marriages which started decades ago in the western countries has reached the Indian society, though here, it is not comparatively as bad yet.

Divorce used to be a disgrace for the family. But it is no longer a bad word. The social stigma attached to it has been diluted to a great extent. Women are now less likely to put up with any shortcomings of their spouses. Instead of staying trapped in unhappy marriages, more and more Indian women prefer to untie the knot and enjoy freedom. Divorce, once a dreaded fate for women in India, seems to be quite acceptable now.

More and more married couples in India are calling it quits. The phenomenon is not restricted to the affluent, urban populace, as it predominantly used to be till as late as 1980s. This trend is spreading to smaller cities and semi-urban areas, as well. Statistics suggest that more and more people from middle and lower middle class are also opting out of unhappy alliances. It is perhaps a reflection of India's changing socio-economic landscape.

Delhi is emerging as the divorce capital of India. In the years 2006 & 2007, approximately 7650 and 8117, divorce/ judicial separation cases were respectively filed in Delhi. The divorce rate in India is still considerably low, as compared to US & UK. As per a recent newspaper report, Britain has more number of divorcees than married couples.[6]

The Delhi Women Commission's recent announcement that it plans to start an exclusive cell for pre-marriage counselling for young couples, mirrors the society's concern about quick break-up of marriages.

China is seeing a similar churning. Even in China, where couples once recited ancient vows "to remain loyal to each other, even if the seas run dry and rocks crumble", are ending marriages these days for the reasons, which were unheard of earlier. Divorce, once unthinkable for women in China, is now viewed almost as a civil right. China's increasing divorce rate is typical of a developing country that is rapidly modernising and becoming affluent. China now has many divorce lawyers, divorce counsellors, pre-nuptial agreements, private detective agencies that photograph cheating spouses. Several TV shows about divorce have become popular in China[7].

Divorcing couples now don't necessarily feel devastated and many look at the end of the marriage, as a new beginning. That's a far cry from the time, when divorcees along with widows were thought inauspicious and shunned by the society. Traditional middle class families are now increasingly embracing the view that it is better to dissolve the 'sacred' union than be in a failed marriage. Education and jobs have made women financially and emotionally secure and they see no reason to continue in unhappy relationships. In a rapidly modernising world, expectations from marriage, too, are changing fast.

Incompatibility, cruelty and adultery are amongst the most commonly cited reasons by those filing for divorce. A large number of them are youngsters. The youth today does not subscribe to the rigid notion of sanctity of marriage as an institution. If things do not work out, they are willing to think of life beyond the matrimonial bond.

A significant change is that more women are filing petitions for dissolution of marriage, something that was unheard of in 70s or 80s. In India, women have always had the legal option to walk out of abusive or unhappy marriage. But mere legal sanction meant little, in view of sanctity attached to the institution of marriage. Now women, who are economically independent and have the backing of their families, are taking charge of their lives; they are exercising their right to divorce, where marriage is not working for them. Rise in divorce rate and its acceptability is also reflected by the fact that now we have a portal to help divorced couples to find a match.

The expectations from marriage have changed. In Indian society earlier, marriage was less about romance and fulfilment of personal fantasies. It was more a way of life, a transition to accept the responsibilities of life. So, when a marriage hit a difficult patch, it was perceived with stoic acceptance and an unquestioned approach of living through the problems. Now, marriage increasingly embodies the culmination of romantic fantasies. It is seen as a fulfilment of personal desires and is delinked from responsibility aspects of family life. Earlier, marriage was about adjustment and adaptability but now, it is more like a power game where both the husband and the wife strive for an equal status.

Growing affluence, 24 × 7 × 365 working lives and paucity of time coupled with greater work mobility and a focus on individual commitments has led to "self" hogging all the space. The continuing need to stand out and not be anonymous and the quest to make 'my own' statement has left spouses with less of time and desire to invest time in working on "the relationship".

Quick break-ups

Statistics show that divorces within the first few years of marriage are on the rise. Going by the trend of more break ups in the early years of marriage, one could say that the proverbial seven-years itch has now narrowed down to 2-3 years. The life of bliss has become shorter. The spark of marriage is now fading earlier. The late marriage may be a reason behind it. A home maker as well as a working wife is experiencing discontentment. The homemaker is comparing herself to the working woman and feels worthless, as she is performing a thankless job. She mourns the loss of her identity. The superwoman, the working woman feels pressured as she is over-performing, because she continues to discharge her traditional role, in addition to her professional duties. Both, the home-maker as well as the working woman, feel pulled in different directions.

Ted Huston, a professor of Human Psychology at the University of Texas in Austin, who studied 168 couples for about 13 years after their wedding day, concluded that the first two years are the key. The changes that take place during this time tell us a lot about where the marriage is headed. The loss of love and affection rather than escalating conflict, was the most salient predictor of distress. Huston noted, "The dominant approach has been to work with couples to resolve conflict, but it should focus on preserving the positive feelings."

While all couples eventually lose a bit of that honeymoon euphoria... those who remain married do not consider this a crushing blow, rather a natural transition from "romantic relationship" to "working partnership...."

The changed expectations from marriage are leading to the trend of walking out of marriage at the slightest friction and maladjustment. Having dreamt of walking into a rainbow with their spouse, youngsters are opting out the moment the rainbow starts to fade. Ancient concept of family values and marital monogamy no longer weigh with younger generation.

Much preparation goes into the performance of marriage as a ritual, Marriage – as an event, where the couple is the star attraction, marriage – as the beginning of the dreamy honeymoon, marriage – as a means to display wealth and prosperity, has taken a centre stage. Marriage has acquired a glamour unrelated to the reality of married life. Whereas, marriage as a relationship, has taken a back seat.

Magazines like "Vivah" have sprung up to exploit the growing fascination with the wedding ritual. At the same time, books like "How to make your marriage work", "Twenty five ways to make your Marriage Hot Again", reflect the concern about increasingly short-lived marriages, and efforts to find ways to make marital bliss last longer.

Second ride: Not a problem

There were times when re-marriage after divorce, especially for women, was formidable. Divorcees had to settle for widowers or older men. The ceremony would be quiet and understated, minus the traditional pomp and pageantry. But now, the pendulum seems to have swung to the other end. Re-marriage ceremonies are planned, even before the ink has dried on the divorce papers. There is none of the restraints associated earlier with second time ceremonies. The stigma of divorce seems to have been conquered. Irrespective of the merits or demerits of short-lived marriages and quick divorces, ridding divorce of stigma is a step in the right direction.

The matrimonial columns show a surfeit of divorced brides and grooms, all fishing in the sea of hope for a second shot at commitment and companionship. There is even a website devoted to matchmaking amongst the second/third timers. Spouses are not apologetic about their failed marriages.

The advent of hope in such generous measures in our lives also means fewer disappointments to contend with. Āshima's marriage had turned out to be a traumatic affair. No sooner had she divorced Harish, she got an eligible groom. Āshima had approached the court for divorce the second time, as her husband suspected that she was still in touch with her ex husband.

Missed the marriage bus? No problem. Whether you are in your mid thirties, late thirties, early forties, fifties or sixties, marriage is always a possibility now. Mindsets are changing as Indians go through a massive cultural and economic renaissance. Their attitudes are shifting from being cautious to being bindās, from being conservative to being experimental.

Premarital sex

A recent study by the Ministry of Women and Child Development revealed that 26.8 per cent young adults (13-18 years) have had their first sexual experience in teenage. For most, it was with classmates and the situation was anything but abusive.[8]

Are the alarm bells ringing now? Can we really blame the children? The young ones now are much more aware of the opposite sex, way before their time. Children are assaulted with explicit sexual images on TV, in movies, and on internet from an early age. They have easy access, most often unsupervised, to information about the adult world of sex. It is no wonder that they are indulging in sex, much earlier than we think they should or would. Premarital sex means sex before maturity. It affects both, the physical as well as mental health.

The Western Story

Western societies are grappling with the rising rate of teenage pregnancies. They have also understood that the solution doesn't lie in stringent laws. Terry Grange, chief constable in the UK police, made headlines recently when he said, "If you prosecute every time a boy has sex with a girl, under age of 16 and above 12, we'd be in school and youth clubs regularly."[9]

The alarming proportion to which the teenage pregnancies have risen can be guessed from a recent move of US schools to go entirely single sex. A school in Green county in Georgia, US has decided to go single sex, in view of high number of teenage pregnancies, besides other reasons.

Recently, a 14-year-old girl gave birth to a full term baby in a bathroom at her Junior High school in Houston, US and then tried to flush it down the toilet, killing the infant.[10]

In yet another recent incident reported by a leading national daily[11], a 14-year-old girl delivered a still born foetus in the bathroom of an airplane on her way back to Houston from a school field trip.

After a survey of more than 6000 people conducted by Kathryn Porter of the National Centre for Health Statistics, US, he concluded that "..... just 4% US adults are virgins. A lot of adults reported their sexual debut at a pretty young age... This is an area of concern because risky sexual behaviour can result in sexually transmitted diseases and unintended pregnancies."

Indian Side

Internet and cable TV has brought exposure to global cultures and life styles. Indian cinema and TV soaps also do not lag behind in exposing Indian youth to global trends. The communication revolution has brought about acceptability of behaviours and life styles, which were unimaginable a few decades ago.

Generation-X perceives its relationships in a very different manner, as compared to their elders. "Sex" is not a big issue. The waning of sexual taboos signals a sea change in attitudes.

What is ridiculous is that our children may well be indulging in consensual sex, while we are still wondering how to impart sex education to them! There may be a situation where parents need counselling more than the children. Whether sex education is to be imparted at home or school may be an irrelevant debate. Children have their own ways of discovering the facts. They are out there doing it, while we are busy figuring out how to tell them! Everyone is advising parents to be liberal and talk about sex to their children, but nobody is telling them how!

The other day, on a routine visit to my gynaecologist, I found a very young couple, may be in the age group of 18-20 years, hanging around in the waiting lounge. "It is surprising to see a boy and a girl married at such a young age these days", I casually remarked.

My doctor gave me a sheepish smile and said, "They are preparing for MBA entrance examination. They have come to Delhi from small townships of Firozabad and Mirzapur and are in the same coaching college in Delhi. They are staying in the same lodging house.... the girl has come for abortion..."

I was shocked. "Don't you counsel such boys and girls?... What if, their parents come to know of it? How would their parents react to it?" I asked.

My gynaecologist then told me, "I do counsel them to the extent that they should stick to one partner. They should use precautions, so that they don't contact any infection and don't land up in similar situation. But I cannot advise beyond that. I can't even think of telling them that they should exercise restraint or should not indulge in sex. Kids are very clear. They want to experience things, in advance". Before I could gather my wits, she told me further, "I get one such case every day. They do not even look hassled. The other day a girl came and disclosed, "It has happened, as that stupid fellow had no experience and could not take care...."

"One case was really amusing. Both came hand in hand and sat before me. The boy took the initiative and told, "Actually I had no such encounter before. She is quite comfortable at it. It's my fault, I suppose! And squeezed the girl's hand with an apologetic look..."

Where does "Sex" figure in the youngsters' scheme of things today, can be visualised from the views expressed by an actor in his interview to a widely read daily. He said, "It's a momentary show of affection. It amounts to satisfying a basic physical need. There's no sleep lost over it. It's not dwelt on for long and the two people involved move on in the morning. Today's generation doesn't credit sex with too much importance. It is incidental and life goes on as before....This new lifestyle apparently has its advantages, especially at a time when urban pressures are making it increasingly difficult to sustain relationships. It helps one to move on. When you want to forget about a person or the past, a casual approach to sex can help you move."[12]

This attitude is not confined only to the elite strata of society. It is now percolating down to the middle class. My friend intentionally broached this topic in presence of her son, who is doing his MBBS internship from Safdarjang Hospital in Delhi. "In my batch only 2-3 girls were cohabiting with classmates. In the new batch, which has just joined, 50% of them are in live-in relationships with fellow batch mates", he shared.

With the arrival of more women, older students and more liberal attitudes, Indian Institute of Management (IIM) campuses are also witnessing something that few talk about openly—live-in relationships in hostels. "In my second year, I shacked up in my girlfriend's room," said Ananya, who earned a Master's in Business Administration from a top-ranking IIM in 2002. He shared that in most IIM hostels, a student gets a room to himself/ herself. So live-in arrangement means that one partner is heading back to his or her room in the morning to get ready for classes. 50 to 70 per cent of the dating couples live together on campus, but do not talk about it. Unlike campus housing in the West, when it comes to the opposite sex, Indian colleges and schools impose hostel curfews and all sort of restrictions. IIMs are an exception, having decided to treat students as adults. "If students cannot manage their own lives, how do you expect them to become leaders?" These were the comments of a spokesman for an IIM[13].

Recently, a national newspaper published the interview of a fashion designer from a middle class family. The designer was cheesed off on a query about her virginity. "It's something very personal to talk about. I could not digest the fact that a fairly educated adult, supposedly of a progressive mindset was inquisitive about my sexuality. Why are young women, who go in for pre-marital sex branded cheap?" she inquired. "It is a very personal decision. Sex is as personal a thing as the institution of marriage. I am interested in someone who is interested in my heart, my thoughts. If he wants to know whether I'm a virgin, he better take a dive in the sea," she said.

It seems that virginity is no longer a noble word, nor is it an expected virtue by most youngsters, and yet parents don't sleep easy till their young ones are home after late night parties. Getting into physical relationships without any commitment, by the younger generation seems to be on the rise.

For the older generation of parents, it is hard to fathom how anyone could share such intimacy casually with one partner and then simply move on to marry someone else.

Premarital sex, takes away the excitement to explore that aspect post–marriage. Earlier, sex after marriage was preceded by effort, more on the part of the male partner, to connect with the spouse. It helped in building emotional bond between the spouses. The excitement associated with physical exploration of each other was "the pleasure". The patient exploration worked to bring man and woman closer. The steady discoveries about each other helped spouses bond psychologically. That excitement has disappeared with premarital sex.

Both, the bride and the groom looked forward to achieving that togetherness. The thrill and excitement of sleeping together after marriage, was a new experience for them which sustained marriage till children were born. After the arrival of baby, the excitement associated therewith kept the couple happy and together. Now couples have eaten the dessert first. There is hardly any excitement to taste that new experience; the couples are also delaying the arrival of child, as both are busy with their careers. As a result, they soon start getting bored of each other's company.

Besides lost excitement, premarital sex leads to other problems as well, like lack of mutual trust, which strikes at the very root of the marital bond. However liberal one may have become, everyone still expects loyalty from the spouse. The moment that is suspect, there are problems.

Interaction with spouses from all walks of life revealed that none of them showed indifference about their partner's sex life. Despite all the talk about wearing one's sexuality on one's sleeve, somewhere down the line, the social milieu does play a part. Even though easy sex appears to be acceptable to Indian youth, it may be just a surface level phenomenon. Where emotions are involved, casual sex may give way to darker emotions of jealousy, possessiveness and resentment. There appears to be a rise in crimes of passion if one goes by media reports.

While there is certainly a change in the attitude of youngsters towards premarital sexual experimentation, nearly 50% of both the boys and girls interviewed in a newspaper survey confessed to being unsure of how would they deal with a situation in which their lover or spouse admits to not being a virgin. Almost two thirds of boys felt virginity was important.

The fact that women are undergoing hymenoplasty/ restoration of hymen or re-virgination surgeries suggests the persistent obsession with female virginity and purity. Even though a large section of men understand and accept that the hymen can be ruptured with physical activity, women still feel compelled to restore the hymen to prove their "purity".

A leading surgeon in this field shared, "Hymenoplasty is common in South American countries, China and Japan. It is only in the last couple of years, that it has gained awareness in India. I have conducted six surgeries in last two years." This gives an impression that we may have come to lead very western lives, but when it comes to marriage and family we get very traditional. This is true of every strata of Indian society.

In India, women continue to be judged on the basis of their past, whereas this does not apply to men. Promiscuity by men is condoned, but women are expected to be the keepers of virtue, which is what drives even urban Indian women to such 'corrective' surgery.

A recent news report 18 talked about the rising trend of hymenoplasty amongst Muslim women in France and other parts of Europe. These women are caught up between the freedom of European society and traditions of their own community and the fear of their parents' and grandparents' generations. For a 23-year-old French student of Moroccan descent from Montpellier, the 30-minute procedure represented the key to a new life: the illusion of virginity. More and more such women are resorting to this cosmetic procedure as it will produce tell-tale vaginal bleeding on wedding night. The whole issue has led to a renewed and fierce debate in France about a prejudice that was supposed to have been buried with the country's sexual revolution 40 years ago : the importance of a woman's virginity.

Dr. Marc Abecassis, a specialist in "intimate" surgery said, "Doctors are empowering patients by giving them a viable future and preventing them from being abused – or even killed – by their fathers or brothers. Who am I to judge? I have colleagues in the US, whose patients do this as a Valentine's present to their husbands. What I do is different. This is not for amusement. My patients don't have a choice if they want to find serenity – and husbands."

Dr. Abecassis mentioned that he performs two to four hymen restorations per week.

There is another trend which seems to have picked up in recent years – that of engaging detectives to verify the background of the love interest. Traditional arranged marriages going in for a background check is an established norm but "in-love" couples tracking backgrounds before the nuptials indicates that love is not so blind to past affairs and involvements.

Sex outside marriage

Twenty two years old Sandy happily agreed to marry a boy of her parent's choice. But within two years of marriage, Sandy was put off by her husband's inability to understand her needs. Sandy looked for answers outside matrimony and found solace in the company of her colleague Samir. An office romance blossomed.

Sandy confided, "We came closer on an official trip to Male. It was a romantic place. The surroundings encouraged proximity. I thoroughly enjoyed Samir's company. The closeness has fructified into a relationship. But I don't regret it... Instead, I feel justified. I missed the intimacy of kisses and hugs in my marriage. There wasn't much closeness between me and my husband. I would come to bed in a sexy nightgown, but he didn't seem to notice it ever. I am an attractive woman, but I was not getting any attention or sex from my husband. Samir's company made me feel beautiful, young and sexy for the first time in the last two years. I really needed it and he knew that I needed it. It was emancipating. I appreciate Samir's limitations, being a married man. I am fine with it."

Seeking fulfillment outside marriage may feel justified, when you convince yourself that you are only filling in some gaps, which are missing in your marriage, so that the marriage does not suffer from that sense of lack (you were feeling). It is a dangerous justification and treads a fine line between balance and disaster.

Trust is the basis of any relationship, including marriage. If not respected, it might lead to terrible results. Entering into a marital relationship is about choosing one person out of many, as your partner. If you go ahead and establish that proximity with someone else, it would amount to cheating on your partner.

Even the suspicion can kill your marriage

Vatsala and Karan belonged to upper middle class. Smart and outgoing, Vatsala had approached the court for divorce, as she was fed up with Karan suspecting her of sharing a physical relationship with her childhood friend. "I was shocked on reaching home after visiting Advait, to find that Karan had made a bonfire of all my expensive dresses out of anger. I lost my head and screamed at him but he was calm as a cucumber. I cannot think of staying with him anymore." said Vatsala.

Karan confided that he was fed up of Vatsala flaunting her proximity with Advait. Though Karan pretended to be broad minded and progressive, he could not tolerate Vatsala's warmth towards Advait.

Vatsalas's closeness to Advait probably hit the trust between them. Karan retaliated by taking revenge. No amount of counselling worked with them. They ultimately parted ways, though amicably.

Resisting temptation

> *He could resist almost anything except temptation.*
>
> *- Oscar Wilde.*

Restraint helps.

A desire to experiment sex casually might kill the excitement of exploring and experiencing it in the intimacy of a committed relationship. It can also leave you feeling used and depressed if the partner moves on without much thought to others, who could also be your own friend. It gets worse, if this happens in a marriage. Casual flings outside a committed relationship/ marriage can prove emotionally devastating for both spouses.

Shane Warne's confession

Shane Warne, the famous Australian spinner, described how he wept as his marriage fell apart over off-field romps with other women. In a frank exchange with top British television interviewer Michael Parkinson, Warne admitted that the marriage break up was his fault. He said, "There were times when I sat by myself and cried. Some of the things that I've done and the mistakes I've made I'm not proud of, but it shows I'm human.... If I had stopped and thought, 'Hang on a minute', I wouldn't have done it. But unfortunately, I gave way to temptation.... I was quite proud of the way I handled the situation because it's never easy going through divorce. It's quite tough and I don't think that anyone realises how hard it is and all the things you have to go through, when you go through divorce." Warne shared, "I haven't ruled out getting back together but we both have to work out (whether) that's what we want. I don't think, we want to get back for the wrong reasons. As I said, we've got three beautiful children together, but we've both got to get back (together) because we both want to.

I still love Simone, I still love my children. I'm a very good parent. I'm a good dad. I mightn't be the best husband, but I'm a good dad and if we can all work that out together and make that work, then great."[14]

Age no bar

It was never a problem for old men to get hitched to women, young enough to be their daughters. The trend seems to be getting reversed with older women being labeled "cradle snatchers" for hooking up with younger men.

From Demi Moore to Zarina Wahab, who married Aditya Pancholi, from Archana Pooran Singh, who married a 6 years younger Parmeet Sethi to Sachin and Anjali Tendulkar, and the most recent match of Abhishek and Aishwarya Bachchan, the celebrity circuit is replete with examples of this reversal of the traditional age gap.

A Delhi based doctor who was heading to marry a colleague eight years older than him disclosed, "Older women are cerebral, bold and know how to express themselves. The brain is the most important sex organ; like in any other relationship, a mental connect is must. If you have that compatibility, the rest falls into place."

Reshmi, a corporate lawyer, who had no qualms in marrying a fellow lawyer five years her junior, noted "Having common interest and sharing the same principles, is more important than a difference in age".

A changed working environment, empowerment of women and an open society have made it easier to go in for such alliances. However, a section of psychologists are expressing concern over such relationships. The sexual urge or prowess of the women, they say, tends to diminish after a certain age. It seems to be a medical fact because the menstruation stops after a certain age. This may lead to incompatibility. That is the stage when such couples may need to be extra sensitive and understanding towards each other.

Being apart–though living together

Working couples who lead hectic stress filled lives, have their own share of problems. Odd working hours, work related travel and juggling multiple responsibilities has taken a toll on libido.

For Rachna and Paul, sex hasn't happened for over a year. "We don't miss it," says Rachna. "We're both caught up in our work, which keeps us apart most of the time. Paul travels quite a bit and I work odd hours. We're not pushing it as we're not ready to have kids as yet." It appears that "sexless marriages" are here to stay and it's only going to get worse over the years, unless there is dramatic change in lifestyle.

Live-in relationship

The Indian woman now has more choices than ever before. These days, women who choose to stay single, cohabit, or date causally are no longer seen as social misfits or rebels, at least in certain strata of society. Opting out of the traditional route of marriage and motherhood is also not seen as a defiance of the system. In these strata, it is considered a choice that women are making for their own reasons.

The concept of bond called marriage forged out of sheer necessity, obligation, or family pressure seems to be on its way out. Increasingly, Indian women (and men) are choosing to date and wait for the right person to come along. A live-in-relationship is a new lifestyle choice.

A report issued by Office for National Statistics, London,[15] revealed that co-habiting is a rising trend in Britain. Another report suggested a 65% increase in couples, who live together but are not married. Office of National Statistics also reported that only 2,36,980 weddings took place in England and Wales in 2006, which was the lowest figure since 1895. It is reported to be the smallest proportion of marriages compared to population, since records began in the mid-Victorian era.

Cohabitation is also common in a small number of advanced societies, some of which – like the Scandinavian countries– give live-in couples the same rights, as those who are legally wed. Marriage, therefore, is often a mere formality, or a matter of choice, in such societies.

As Indians became exposed to global cultures and influences, change was inevitable. The institution of marriage itself is gradually being put to test in contemporary Indian society, more so in urban pockets. More couples than ever before are opting not to tie the knot, preferring to simply live together instead.

'Salaam Namaste', starring Preity Zinta and Saif Ali Khan, a story based on a 'live-in-relationship', was, I think, the first Bollywood movie showcasing a 'live-in" situation between a boy and a girl. It mirrored the existing state of things.

The concept of live-in relationship has come to India from the West, where it came to be accepted because of very peculiar reasons. In West, children are on their own once major. Accustomed to a life of total freedom, young boys and girls not wanting to get chained into a marital bond took to this alternative. Also, due to high pressure jobs, the percentage of marriages and children are on the decline in certain western countries, to the extent that some countries have experienced negative growth of population. Western society thus does not mind, if couples lived-in and have children. Another major reason for the popularity of this convenience called live-in-relationship is heavy cost of breakup of marriage by way divorce settlements.

Live-in relationships are happening in India, but the numbers are still small, and concentrated in the metros. India is still very traditional and often, couples refrain from telling their parents about their live-in relationships, for fear of offending their value systems. Preity Zinta who portrayed this life style in 'Salaam Namaste' reportedly remarked that "she would never do it in real life because she believes in the institution of marriage."[16]

"Marriage is popular because it combines the maximum of temptation with the maximum of opportunity."

- George Bernard Shaw

Marriage is preferred in India

Thanks to a combination of social and religious factors, as well as the absence of safety net and welfare measures, marriage is still an institution that is preferred over any other form of union. We need to take note that changes are taking place, even in India. Instead of ruing the loss of old values, we would be better off gearing up for new realities, which includes updating our laws and social attitudes.

Whether living-in is liberating or harmful to marriage? What are the benefits and drawbacks of staying single and what are the repercussions of casual sex? These might be the concerns of older generations, but an upwardly mobile younger generation especially, women, are choosing from many relationship choices. No matter what choice a woman makes, the important thing is that she now goes into it with complete self-awareness and for her own reasons.

Downside of live-in relationship

Live-in relationships appeal to romantic instincts. Couples are so much in love that they move in together. They can't seem to spend time away from each other. However, sustaining a live-in relationship may not be easy. In the long run, it turns out to be like a marital relationship, but without the social and legal safeguards built into a marriage. Then there is the challenge of dealing with the traditionalists of society.

The level of commitment in a live-in relationship tends to be less, though there may be exceptions. Amrita Pritam is a notable exception. She had a long lasting relationship with her partner Imtiaz, without the formality of marriage. But their relationship was not openly discussed in literary circles, while she was alive.

Low commitment in such relationships may be attributed to the fact that in marriage, your family is also a part of the whole affair. Involvement of parents and family, on both sides, bring in social pressure to honour the commitment. Studies on this subject have reported that the risk sharing between individuals in a non-marital relationship is almost negligible. Irrespective of the authenticity of these studies, this fact finds support in the basic human nature. As there is a minimal or no commitment in this kind of relationship, so persons may not find it worthwhile to take risk for the live-in companion.

Anyone contemplating such a move needs to be mindful of certain things, lest they end up feeling shortchanged. Your live-in mate is not your husband nor is responsible as such. Indian law doesn't recognise "live in relationships." Under the Protection of Women from Domestic Violence Act, 2005, one can claim compensation for abuse by a boyfriend. Otherwise, if a live in relationship is over, neither party can claim maintenance or in fact any kind of monetary payment from the other. For that you have to be married or be able to prove an "implicit marriage", which one may find difficult to prove.

Before opting for a live-in relationship, it is advisable to make sure that both the partners are committed to the relationship; it should not be viewed purely as a matter of convenience. The couple has to be emotionally mature and geared to deal with opposition from family, colleagues, neighbours, and society. Cohabitation may affect the relationship with parents, because in a majority of families, cohabitation is still considered morally wrong and embarrassing to the extended family members. Cohabitors from such families risk damaging their relationship with their parents and experiencing the withdrawal of parental and extended family support for the relationship.

For live-in-relationship to work, it is very important that both the partners respect each other's space within the relationship and do not take each other for granted.

One bright spot in this relationship is that it is easier to dissolve than a marriage because of the lack of legal tangles and implications, and also because those who live-in often, prefer not to have children. Another heartening fact revealed by some studies is that cohabiting couples are far more likely than those who are married, to split housework evenly. But after wedding, they revert to the stereotype, with the woman taking on the majority of tasks. A woman may find that the kind and considerate man, she lived with for years suddenly stops helping her with mopping, dusting, washing and sharing other chores. It is probably because the couple has got married. Cohabitors, therefore, may be more prone to aggressive bargaining when it comes to exchanges of time and effort in the household, and less willing to do more than what they perceive as their fair share.

Anna Addison, 30, who lives in Middlesbrough with her husband Paul, said, "When we first moved in, the novelty of living together meant we shared the housework. It was the same for the first year after we got married, but when I got a nine-to-five job everything was left to the weekends and I ended up doing it all myself.

... Paul definitely changed after marriage. I do rely on him for some technical things in the house but, for housework, it's just me now."[17]

Bluntly put, there may be no commitment in cohabitation. But the likelihood of a more peaceful relationship is higher than in a marriage. It is also seen that when the marriage takes place, the race is over. Men see the need to behave as starting to diminish.

Cohabiting vs Marriage

The love that we all want from the partner may not be possible without both having the commitment to try to make it last. As marriage is considered to be for life-time, it encourages emotional investment in the relationship. In contrast, cohabitation might mean, "I will be here only as long as the relationship meets my needs."

Children's emotional development is felt to be poorer, if a parent is cohabiting; it is greater and healthier, if a parent is married. It is partly because of the high risk that the couple might break up. If the couple does separate, the children pay an economic, as well as, emotional price, since they may not get legal support from a partner who is not their biological parent. They would also lose a caring adult, who may have taken a parental role but will do so no longer.

In a recent case, the Supreme Court has observed that a man and a woman who have lived in for a long period of time could be considered, as good as married. Children born of such relationships will be considered legitimate. The court upheld the property rights of a woman who was born to a live-in couple from Madhya Pradesh. But this verdict does not in any manner validate a live-in relationship.

Compared to singles or live-in partners, married people as a group, are emotionally happier. Married couples are better connected to the larger community, including in-laws and other social groups, who provide social and emotional support and material benefits. Surprisingly, one of the studies even mentioned that the married couples have better sex lives than cohabitors, as there is no fear in it. Although cohabitor might have sex at least, as often as married ones, but they are less likely to say they enjoy it. Because, marriage adds the essential ingredients of commitment and security to one's sex life, making it more satisfying. Married couples are more likely than cohabitors to perceive love and sex as intrinsically connecting.

Some studies have also suggested that cohabiting women are more likely than married women to suffer physical and sexual abuse. Aggression is estimated to be at least twice as common among cohabits, as it is among married couples.

Married men make more effort to have increased earnings than single men. This may be explained by the increased financial responsibility men feel when they marry; many men have been heard saying "marriage made me serious about my career and making a good living."

Does living-in together before marriage not resemble taking a car for a test drive? If you don't get the kick in the drive, you have the option of kicking it out.

Living apart together (LAT)

Some couples have separate bedrooms. Others go a step further and have separate households even though they are living in a committed relationship. This trend, known as Living Apart Together (LAT), is catching on in German Cities, according to a new study by Berlin's Humboldt University.

"It has become particularly popular with couples in their late 30s. They see this as an attractive and long-term alternative to a conventional relationship, unlike younger couples who often view it as a temporary solution," said a researcher.

Research showed that LAT couples were just as happy, as those who shared a home together, especially if they were independent, both personally and financially.

Bigitte Daniel and her boyfriend, Peter lived in an LAT

relationship for four years, after which both went through failed marriages and cohabiting relationship. "It worked out very well," says Daniel, who kept a three room apartment in a Hamburg suburb, while Peter lived in his own house just outside the north German port city.

The couple, both in their early 50s, recently decided to move in together, after Daniel lost the job and could no longer afford the rent for her apartment.

Older couples in India may have been LAT couples unknowingly, since ages. My friend's parents did not get along very well. But they did not seek divorce. Her father most of the time stayed at their Delhi home; her mother stayed in Shimla, where she was working as the principal of a school. Same was the case with Rashmi's parents. Her father lived with her elder brother, whereas her mother lived with the youngest one. Both chose to live apart. But that was more of a family arrangement and to help children.

***

- ♥ There is rise in age of marriage; duration of marriage has shortened.
- ♥ Girls and boys are now more choosy; mental compatibility and material comforts weigh more.
- ♥ Rise in divorce rate indicates heightened expectations from marriage.
- ♥ Second marriage is not much of a problem any more.
- ♥ Premarital sex is more prevalent now; although while choosing the partner still the same value is attached to 'virginity'.
- ♥ Sex outside marriage may thrill – but kills the relationship.
- ♥ 'Live–in' relationship is now a choice being made amongst upper strata.
- ♥ LAT- existed in India since ages – though not so defined.

8

MISCELLANY

Go green in love: Save global warming

Divorce not only proves disastrous for children but is also bad for the environment. It contributes to global warming. Does this sound ridiculous? It is no joke. Recent research in the US made this claim!

Scientists at Michigan State University reported in the proceedings of the National Academy of Sciences that the global trend towards higher divorce rate has created more households with fewer people. More households mean more energy expended to build, towards fuel and to provide water for them. They say that globally, the number of households is increasing much faster than the number of people. Even in regions with declining population, there is a substantial increase in the number of households. They conclude that divorce is the main reason for reducing the number of people in a household. Whether there are two or three or six people in a house, the amount of fuel needed for heating is about the same.

Researchers also found that divorce tosses out any economies of scale. In the United States, divorced households used 73 billion kilowatt-hours of electricity and 62,700 crore gallons of water in 2005 that could have been saved, if households had stayed the same size as when they were married. Thirty-eight million extra rooms were needed with associated costs for heating and lighting.

As per the study, in the United States and 11 other countries such as Brazil, Costa Rica, Ecuador, Greece, Mexico and

South Africa between 1998 and 2002, if divorced households had combined to have the same average household size as married households, there could have been 7.4 million fewer households.

The number of divorced households in those countries ranged from 40,000 in Costa Rica to almost 16 million in the United State around 2000. The number of rooms per person in divorced households was 33% to 95% greater than in married households.

Isn't it worth sparing a thought before breaking a marriage, may be for humanity's sake?

Economics of love

A study conducted by the Centre for Policy Dialogue (CPD), Bangladesh, reported that Taka 342,397.7 million, which was roughly 10 percent of the gross domestic product (GDP) of Bangladesh was spent every year for care of tortured or injured spouses, on their medical treatment, shelter and legal actions[1].

As per the study, of the total cost associated with violence against women by their husbands, Taka 131,180.7 million or 4.1% of the GDP was spent on medical treatment of the injured or traumatised wives. The women victims needed to spend Taka 17,917 million covering treatment, displacement, arbitration, civil legal service, criminal justice and lost working days, due to spousal violence per head per year. India must not be behind on this score though, such data is not available.

The finding that 10 per cent of the country's GDP was being wasted due to "spousal violence" has made the Government of Bangladesh sit up and take notice. Marital conflict and domestic violence has forced the Bangladesh government to take immediate measures to address the problem. The Bangladesh government now plans to include "domestic violence" as a subject in the school curriculum. "We plan to have the subject on "domestic violence" in the primary textbooks to make people aware about it from their childhood," said Women and Children Affairs adviser of the interim cabinet, Rasheda K Chowdhury. Bangladesh Government also impressed upon the political parties to declare their specific plan to prevent gender violence, as the country was set to witness the general elections.

Would not husbands and wives in India, like to contribute to the GDP and help our economy grow?

***

- ♥ Save marriage – save energy and other resources.
- ♥ Promote love – help better utilisation of national income.

REFERENCES

Chapter 1

1. "In defence of marriage" by Balvinder, The Tribune, 27 Nov'2005.
2. "Urge to splurge : weddings, birthdays get fancier" – Anubha Sahni Joshi – Times of India
3. Harbour Bridge - Times of India – 4th June'2008
4. "The Science of a Happy Marriage" - Michael Gurian – Reader's Digest – Nov'2004.
5. "UK TV preaches arranged marriage"- Times of India.

Chapter 2

1. "When should you call it quits" – Vinta Nanda – Times of India, Sunday Times, 15th July'2007.
2. "Financial Compatibility behind Wedded bliss" – Tara Siegel Bernard – Times of India – 13th Sept'2008.
3. Unloading leftovers of past loves by uploading them – Rebecca Cathcart – Times of India.
4. "Hiding success to keep boyfriend" - Tony Allen Mills – Times of India - 2nd Oct'2007.

Chapter 3

1. Secrets About Women Husbands Should Know – Beth Levine- Reader's Digest- Sept'99
2. "A soothing touch helps" – Rouge – Times of India – 13th Sept'2008.
3. Did you touch someone today – Vinita Dawra Nangia – Times Life, Times of India, 29th July 2007.

4. "Beware of These 5 obstacles in your marriage" – Sabina Kadereit Reader's Digest, Oct'2001
5. "Why Men Lie and Women Cry" – Allan and Barbara Pease
6. "Retired husband syndrome"-Anthony Faiola – The Tribune- 20th Oct'2005.
7. "Best of both worlds" - Times Life, Times of India, 2nd March'2008.
8. "Tit for Tat affairs wreck marriages in Malaysia"- Times of India – 24th July'2007.
9. "China gets over dread of divorce" – Jim Yardley – Times of India – 5th Oct'2005.
10. "Woman Posts Evidence of Hubby's Adultery Online – Times of India – 14th August'2008.

Chapter 5

1. " Happy marriage is all about training of a different kind" – Amy Sutherland – Indian Express – 1st July'2006.
2. "Is that really so?" – Vinita Dawra Nangia – Times Life - Times of India , 4th May 2008.

Chapter 6

1. "MARITAL SPATS TAKEN TO HEART" – Denise Gellene – Indian Express – 6th Oct'2007.
2. Ibid.

Chapter 7

1. "NETRIMONY" – Damyanti Datta - India Today 24th March' 2008
2. Ibid
3. Ibid
4. Ibid
5. Ibid
6. " Divorcees outnumber married couples in UK" - Times of India, June 2008.
7. "China gets over dread of divorce" – Jim Yardley – Times of India – 5th Oct'2005
8. "Sex & the Teen" Haimanti Mukherjee and Susmita Mukherjee

"What's Hot" - Times of India - 8th June 2007
9. Ibid
10. "Girl delivers in school, flushes baby" - Times of India - 4th April'2008.
11. Ibid
12. " Just friends, just sex" - Delhi Times, The Times of India - 6th June'2007.
13. " Indian Institute of Live – in Management" - Aparna Kalra – Hindustan Times, 19th Dec'2007.
14. " Break-up made Warne weep" - Times of India" - 9th Jan'2007.
15. " In UK, married couple could soon be in minority" - Times of India - 6th Oct'2007.
16. "In defence of marriage" - by Balvinder – The Tribune - 27th Nov'2005.
17. " In US, men do less housework after marriage" - Roger Dobson & Roger Waite – Times of India - 13th Aug'2007

Chapter 8

1. "Fighting couples lost 10pc of GDP" – PTI – Times of India – 11th Aug'2008.

Others:

1. "Do you really want to know?" – Vinita Dawra Nangia – Times of India – 4th Nov'2007.
2. "Love is forever!" – Times of India – 23rd Oct'2005.
3. "Individualism in the future : American style for Indian ishtyle"- Hamsini Shivakumar – Economic Times, 24th July 2007.
4. "Get Even Closer – what's the key? It's simple and not what you think" - Pamela Redmord Satran – Reader's Digest – Dec'2002.
5. " Will your marriage last" - Aviva Patz – Reader's Digest – January 2001
6. Answered Life's Toughest Questions – Jeanne Marie Laskas – Reader's Digest - April'2006

***

ACKNOWLEDGMENTS

I thank my editor from the depth of my heart for his valuable suggestions which helped me improve upon the manuscript.

I am deeply indebted to my father, Dr. Janak Raj Jai, who pestered me endlessly to record my court experiences in my personal diary. I thank him no less for inspiring me to go beyond my (official) duty and to delve deeper into the psyche of troubled souls/spouses.

Maninder, my friend takes the credit of encouraging me to convert my diary into this book. Her confidence in me reassured me that I can undertake this task. She enthused me to bring it to an end. Her patient repeated readings of my work and her critical comments were invaluable. Her contribution defies exact description.

Mona aka Seema Uniyal, another friend of mine added literary flavour to this book. I was touched by the keen interest she took in my work and the way she put across mildly, the suggestions which helped me immensely. I have no words to thank her for contributing a small poem for this book.

Pushpanjali, my son Apoorv's friend really impressed me with her clarity of thoughts for her age and her creativity. Her instant reaction that titles of the Chapters and the sub-heads, were too revealing, set me rethinking. Despite her hectic college schedule and other activities she is involved in, she took out time and helped me refine my work.

My sons Apoorv & Ishaan and my husband Anil were with me throughout this venture. Their contribution by sparing me for this work is immeasurable. Their random comments on my work made me realise that they evinced great interest in my work. Their encouragement kept me going and pushed me to bring this book to an end.

My younger son, Ishaan, a computer wizard helped me with downloads of quotes and poems on the subject from the internet and in my search for other material on the subject.

I thank no less, the husbands and the wives litigating before me, who were the real inspiration; who set me thinking about this relationship seriously. I am also indebted to the spouses who shared their stories and revealed honestly, the dark side of their relationship.

I also owe a debt of gratitude to many others, whose names could not be accommodated here for reasons of space, but without whose support and assistance, this book would not have been possible.

***